DK Pocket Gen

MAMMALS

FACTS AT YOUR FINGERTIPS

LONDON, NEW YORK, MUNICH,
MELBOURNE, and DELHI

DK DELHI
Project editor Megha Gupta
Project art editor Pooja Pawwar
Senior editor Kingshuk Ghoshal
Senior art editor Rajnish Kashyap
Editor Esha Banerjee
DTP designers Jaypal Singh, Sachin Singh
Picture researcher Sakshi Saluja
Managing editor Alka Thakur Hazarika
Managing art editor Romi Chakraborty
CTS manager Balwant Singh
Production manager Pankaj Sharma

DK LONDON
Senior editor Fleur Star
Senior art editor Rachael Grady
US editor Margaret Parrish
US senior editor Rebecca Warren
Jacket editor Manisha Majithia
Jacket designer Laura Brim
Jacket manager Sophia M. Tampakopoulos Turner
Production editor Lucy Sims
Production controller Mary Slater

Publisher Andrew Macintyre
Associate publishing director Liz Wheeler
Art director Phil Ormerod
Publishing director Jonathan Metcalf

Consultant Dr. Kim Dennis-Bryan

TALL TREE LTD.
Editors Camilla Hallinan, Joe Fullman, Jon Richards
Designer Ed Simkins

First American Edition, 2013

Published in the United States by
DK Publishing
375 Hudson Street,
New York, New York 10014

13 14 15 16 17 10 9 8 7 6 5 4 3 2 1
001–187502–Jun/13

Published in Great Britain by Dorling Kindersley Limited.

A catalog record for this book
is available from the Library of Congress.

ISBN: 978-1-4654-0884-6

Printed and bound in China by South China Printing Company

CONTENTS

Scales and sizes
The book contains profiles of mammals with scale drawings to show their size.

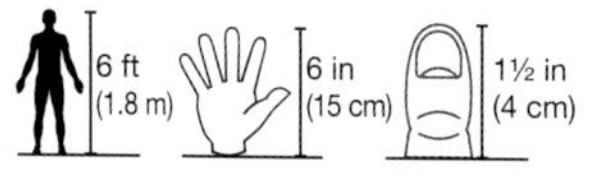

Endangered mammals
This label indicates that the mammal is in danger of dying out.

ENDANGERED

What is a mammal?

A mammal is an animal that has body hair and feeds its young on milk produced by the female's mammary glands. This diverse group of animals is made up of more than 5,000 species.

Mammal features

Like all mammals, this polar bear is warm-blooded—it can control its body temperature internally. Mammals also share some other common features.

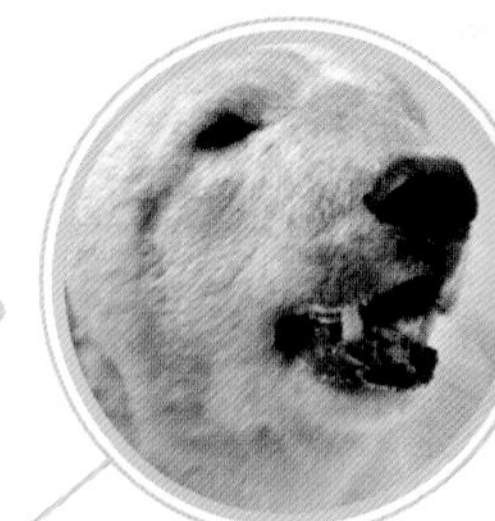

The **lower jaw** of every mammal is made of a single bone called the dentary, which hinges with the skull.

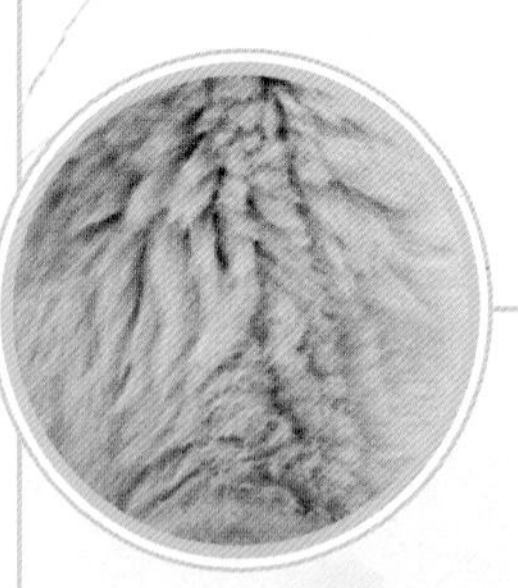

Most mammals have a dense **coat of hair** called fur covering their bodies. This helps to keep them warm.

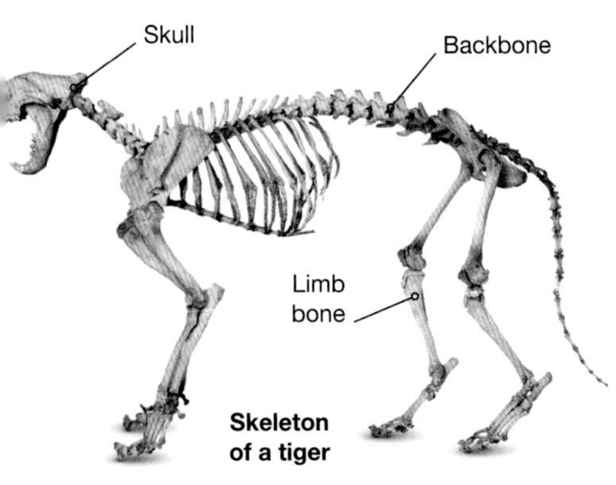

Skeleton of a tiger

Anatomy

In spite of their incredible diversity, all mammals have the same kinds of bones. The bones vary mainly in shape and size from one mammal to another. The flipper bones of a whale, for example, are similar to the limb bones of this tiger.

SPECIAL ADAPTATIONS

Although most mammals live on land, some live in water, while others can take to the air. Over millions of years, these mammals have evolved unique body shapes that allow them to swim or fly.

Aquatic mammals, such as whales, dolphins, and porpoises, live under water. They swim using flippers, which evolved from the limbs of their land-living ancestors.

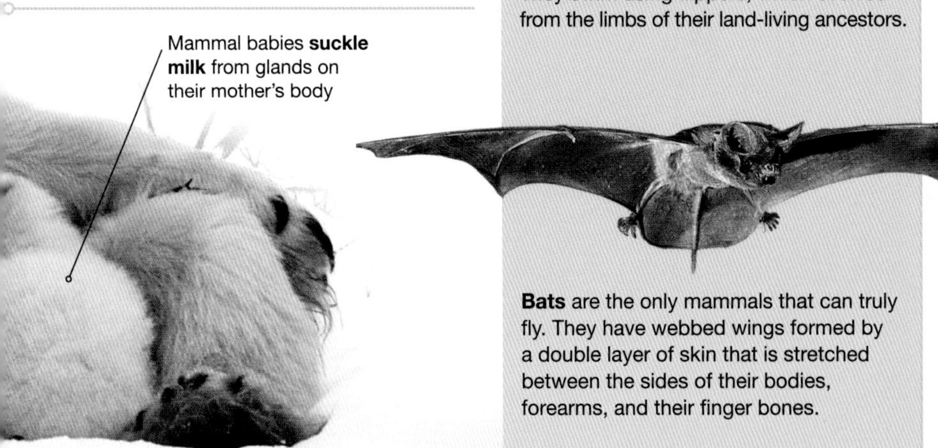

Mammal babies **suckle milk** from glands on their mother's body

Bats are the only mammals that can truly fly. They have webbed wings formed by a double layer of skin that is stretched between the sides of their bodies, forearms, and their finger bones.

Mammal evolution

Mammals first appeared about 220 million years ago and then developed into many different forms. Over millions of years, small changes in how they looked and behaved gave them an advantage that favored their survival over their reptile ancestors.

Mammal evolution

The first mammals, such as this *Sinoconodon*, lived in a world dominated by dinosaurs. These mammals were rat-sized and could scurry around unnoticed. They were also warm-blooded and hairy—features that kept them warm, allowing them to hunt at night when it was too cold for many dinosaurs to be active.

Evolving skull

Reptile jaws are made of many bones, but a single bone called the dentary makes up the lower jaw of mammals. Mammals evolved different kinds of teeth for biting, gripping, tearing, and grinding their food, which helped them to obtain more nutrients. Reptiles, however, have just one kind of teeth and simply grab and gulp in their food.

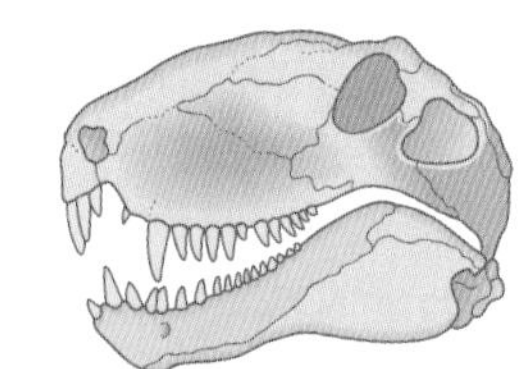

Early reptile

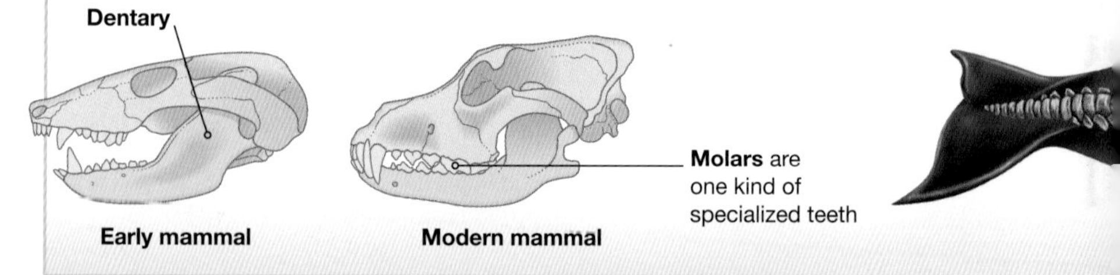

Early mammal

Modern mammal

Whale evolution

When the dinosaurs died out about 65 million years ago, mammals were able to flourish in most habitats in the absence of larger predators. Mammals larger than rat-sized creatures gradually evolved. The ancestors of the whales walked on land about 55 million years ago. Over millions of years, their forelimbs evolved into finlike flippers and their bodies became longer, streamlined, and more suited to living in water.

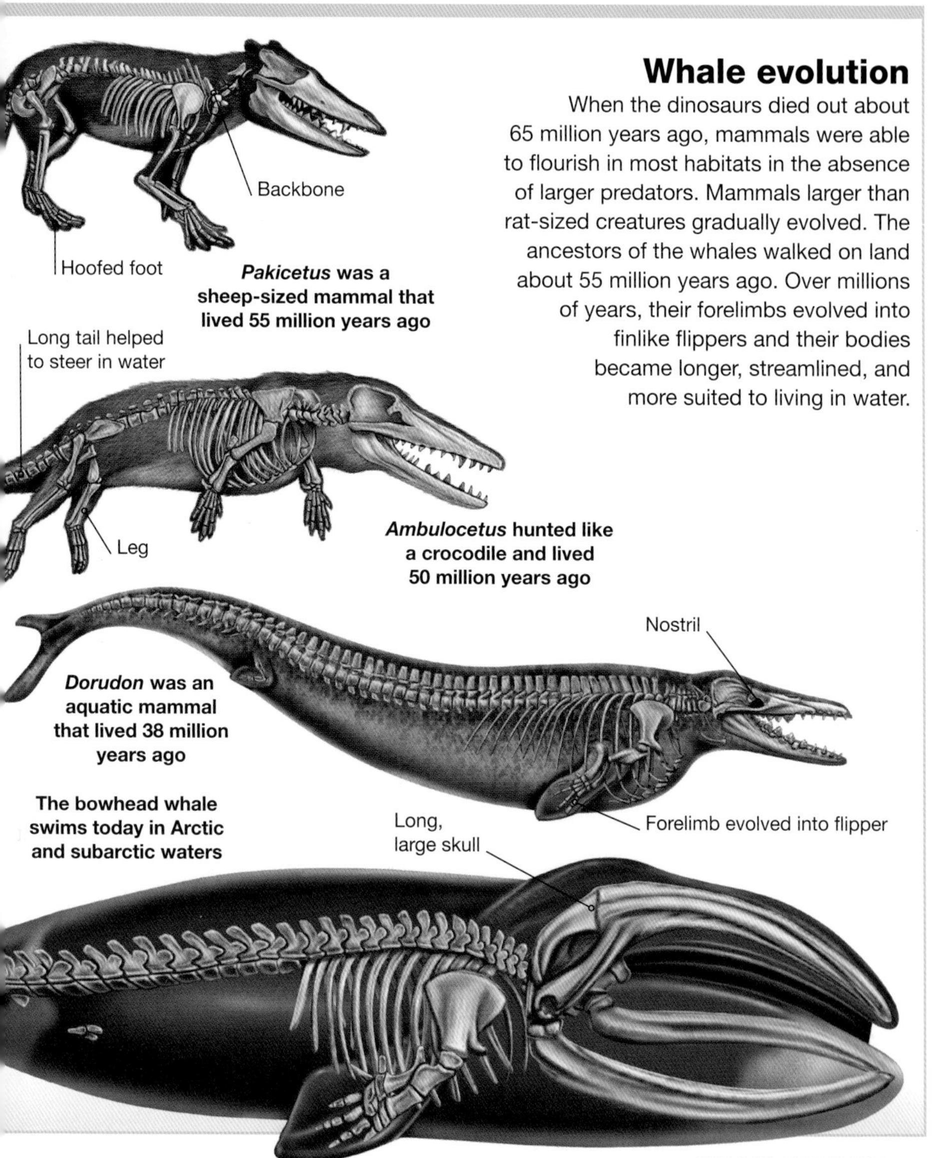

Pakicetus **was a sheep-sized mammal that lived 55 million years ago**

Ambulocetus **hunted like a crocodile and lived 50 million years ago**

Dorudon **was an aquatic mammal that lived 38 million years ago**

The bowhead whale swims today in Arctic and subarctic waters

Feeding and diet

Mammals need energy to survive and they obtain it by eating food. Some eat plants, others eat animals, and some eat both. Most mammals need to find food every day and use different senses to search for it.

Finding food

Mammals use a variety of senses to find food. Wolves have a keen sense of smell, bushbabies can see clearly in even the smallest amounts of light, and some moles can feel their way to their prey. Some species have developed creative ways of getting their food. Chimpanzees, for example, use twigs as tools to dig termites out of their nests.

Different diets

Many mammals stick to certain types of food—such as fruit, leaves, nectar, meat, or carcasses—and can be described according to their diet.

Meat-eaters, such as this sea lion, are also called **carnivores**.

Plant-eaters are called **herbivores**. Plants are not rich in nutrients, so herbivores, such as cows, need to eat large amounts of food to get enough nutrition. Animals that eat both plants and meat are called **omnivores**.

Storing food

Some mammals, such as hamsters and chipmunks, hoard food to prepare themselves for seasons when food is in short supply. Other mammals, such as leopards, store their kill on the branches of trees to keep it safe from other ground-dwelling predators, such as hyenas.

A half-eaten carcass of a springbok can weigh up to 90 lb (40 kg)

Attack and defense

The natural world is full of danger for many mammals as predators can strike at any time. They may chase down their prey, before catching and killing it with their claws and teeth. For mammals being preyed upon, fleeing is often the best option, but moving in a group may also help in defense.

High-speed hunters

Some predators hide and wait for prey before ambushing it, while others chase after prey at high speeds. The cheetah is the fastest land-based predator and chases after prey, such as this gazelle, at a top speed of 71 mph (114 kph). When close enough, it trips up its prey before biting its throat and suffocating it.

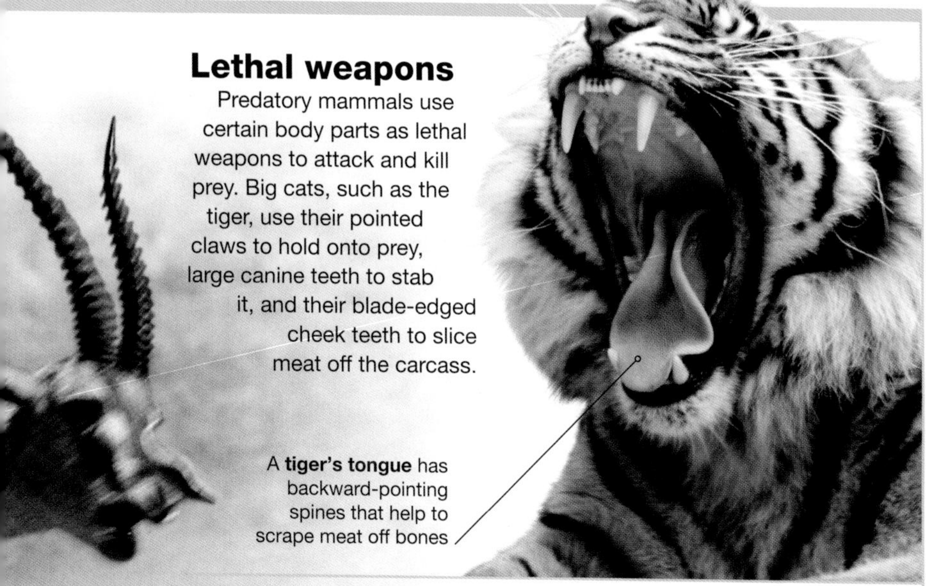

Lethal weapons

Predatory mammals use certain body parts as lethal weapons to attack and kill prey. Big cats, such as the tiger, use their pointed claws to hold onto prey, large canine teeth to stab it, and their blade-edged cheek teeth to slice meat off the carcass.

A **tiger's tongue** has backward-pointing spines that help to scrape meat off bones

Safety in numbers

Living in a group helps some mammals, such as zebras, to avoid capture. When a predator gives chase, the dazzling stripes on zebras may appear as a mass of moving lines to the hunter, confusing it. This may cause it to lose focus on the zebra it has singled out.

Habitats

The environment in which a mammal lives is called its habitat. Mammals live in a wide variety of habitats on land, including tropical forests, deserts, and grasslands, as well as in the seas and oceans.

The air is very low in oxygen high up in the **mountains**, making it difficult for animals to breathe. The mountain goat has a large number of red blood cells, which help it to absorb more oxygen from the air.

Isolated mammals

Lemurs are found only on the island of Madagascar. In the absence of monkeys and apes on the island, they had little competition for food and other resources and so flourished. Some grew to large sizes—at least one extinct species was larger than a gorilla.

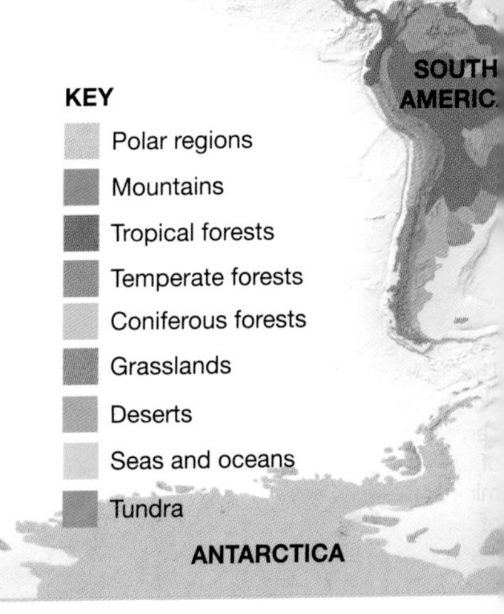

Polar regions have brief, cold summers and long, freezing winters. The thick, furry coat of the polar bear keeps it warm in these conditions.

Most trees in **temperate forests** shed their leaves in the winter and grow new ones in the spring. The red deer feeds on bark from trees in the winter and feeds on the new leaves in the summer.

The beluga whale has a streamlined body. This lets it swim easily through **seas and oceans**.

The light-colored skin of the dromedary camel reflects some of the Sun's rays, minimizing the amount of heat it absorbs in a hot **desert**.

Trees in **tropical forests** grow to great heights and have dense foliage. Mammals such as the fossa are skilled climbers and often hunt in the foliage.

Grasslands don't offer much cover for mammals to hide. Running swiftly is often the best way to seize prey or escape predators. Kangaroos hop away at speeds of up to 40 mph (65 kph) to escape danger.

Types of mammal

Living mammals are divided into 29 orders, which are groups of closely related families of species. These orders are grouped into three major categories based on how the mammals reproduce—egg-laying, pouched, and placental.

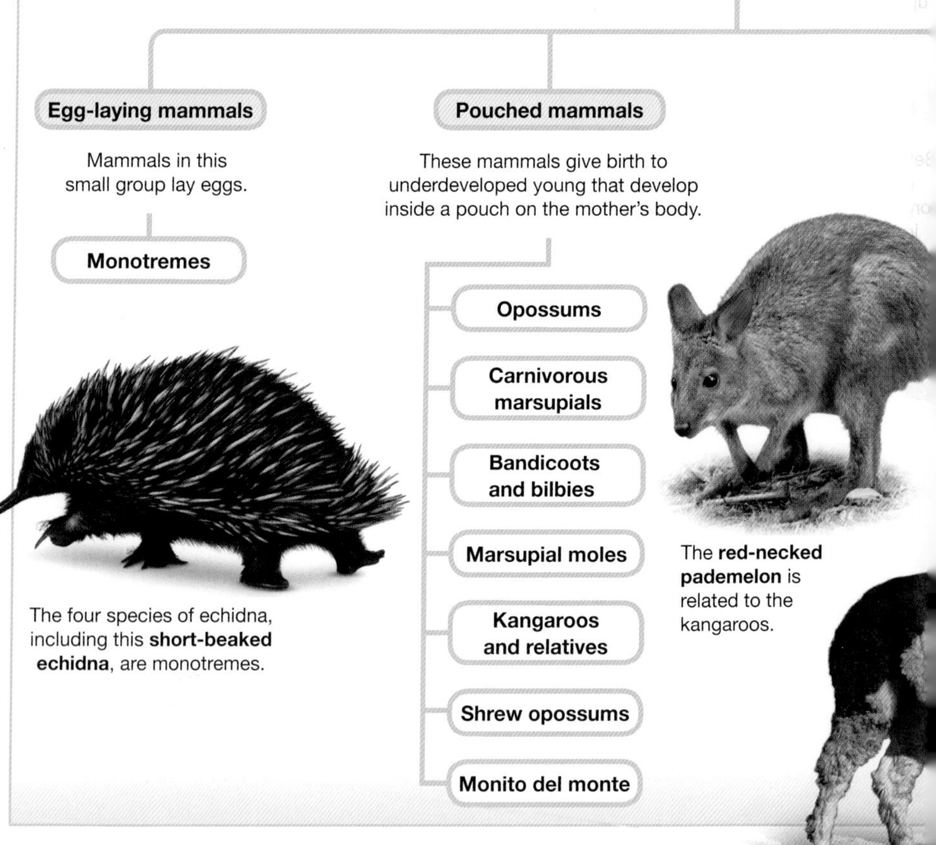

The four species of echidna, including this **short-beaked echidna**, are monotremes.

The **red-necked pademelon** is related to the kangaroos.

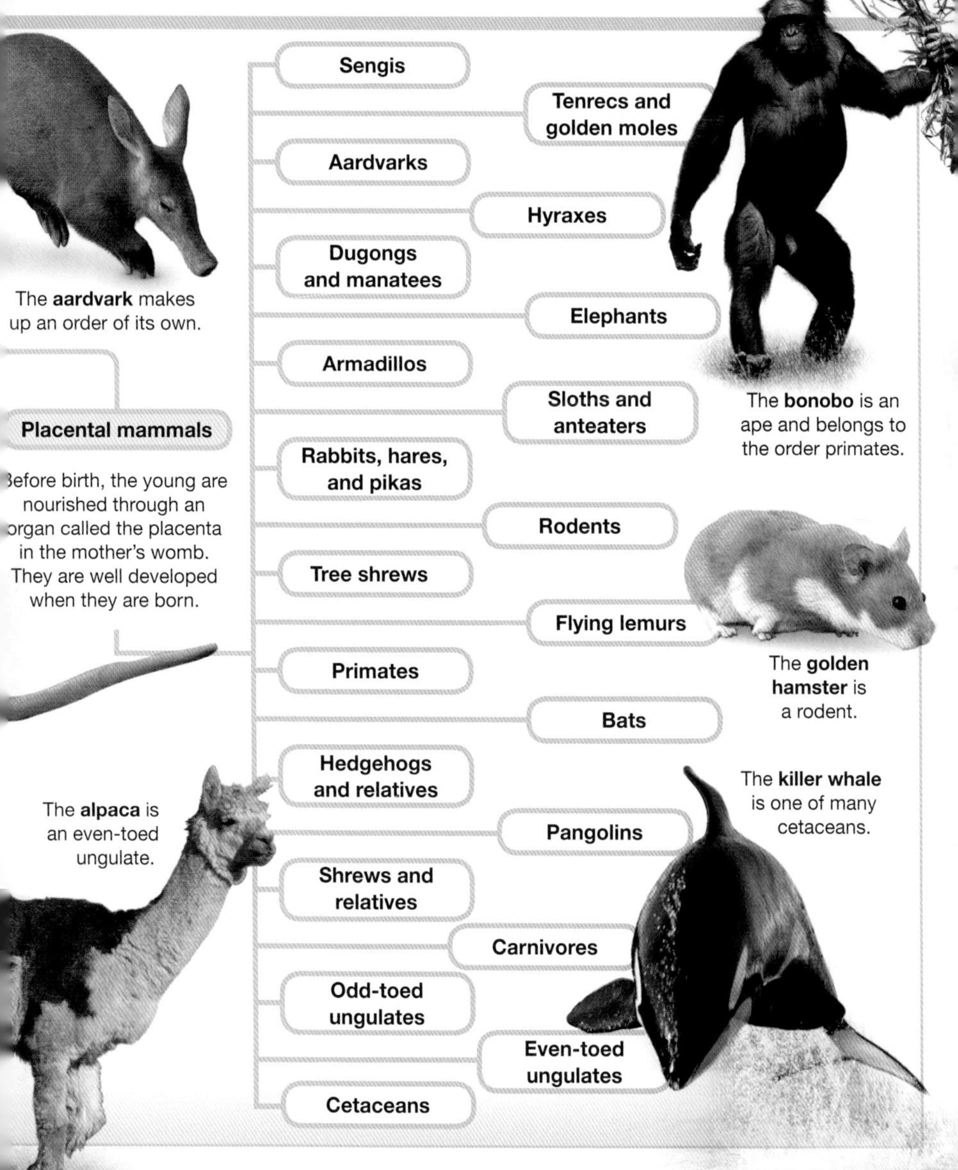

The **aardvark** makes up an order of its own.

Before birth, the young are nourished through an organ called the placenta in the mother's womb. They are well developed when they are born.

The **alpaca** is an even-toed ungulate.

The **bonobo** is an ape and belongs to the order primates.

The **golden hamster** is a rodent.

The **killer whale** is one of many cetaceans.

Conservation and extinction

Many wild mammals are victims of illegal hunting, uncontrolled felling of trees, and other kinds of habitat change caused by human activities. More than one-fifth of the world's mammals are endangered, and in the years to come, many more are likely to become so.

Extinct mammals

Some species have died out mainly because of human activities. Farmers in Australia mistakenly thought that the thylacine, or the Tasmanian tiger, was killing their sheep and began to hunt it. The last Tasmanian tiger died in 1936 and the species became extinct.

Endangered mammals

The International Union for Conservation of Nature (IUCN) is an organization that was formed in 1948 to carry out a range of activities to protect wildlife and animal habitats. It regularly compiles a list of species—called the Red List—based on the level of risk of extinction the animals are facing. Those that face the possibility of extinction in the future are categorized as "endangered" and those that are currently in danger of becoming extinct are called "critically endangered."

The **black rhinoceros** is critically endangered. Poachers kill the animals and cut off their horns, which are used to make medicines

Conservation

Organizations and individuals often rescue endangered mammals and move them to a safer environment where they can live and thrive. National parks, for example, protect the natural habitats of many mammals and save the animals from threats such as illegal hunting.

Protecting mammals Scientist Jane Goodall is seen here with an orangutan. Inspired by her 45-year-long study of chimpanzees, she founded the Jane Goodall Institute that works toward the protection of habitats of apes and other animals.

The critically endangered **red wolf** used to be trapped and killed because it was considered a threat to livestock in North America.

Clearing of the **eastern gorilla**'s forest habitat in Africa has caused its numbers to fall so that it is now endangered.

Europe's **Iberian lynxes** depend on rabbits for food. A fall in the number of rabbits has made this lynx critically endangered.

Just **1,600**

giant pandas exist in the wild today

GIANT PANDA
Since 1961, the giant panda has been the symbol of WWF, an organization that works for the conservation of the natural world. The panda is endangered because its forest habitat in China is being destroyed for lumber and farmland.

Egg-laying mammals

Monotremes, or egg-laying mammals, such as this echidna, make up a small group of mammals found in various habitats in New Guinea, Australia, and Tasmania. They are the only mammals that lay eggs. Once an egg hatches, the baby feeds on milk produced by the mother's mammary glands.

SENSITIVE BILL
The bill of the duck-billed platypus is covered in sensitive skin. Electrical receptors on the skin detect invertebrates, even in murky water.

Egg-laying mammals

The mammals in this group are also called monotremes (meaning "one hole") because their digestive, urinary, and reproductive systems end in a single opening called the cloaca. Monotremes form one of the oldest groups of mammal and are believed to have evolved more than 120 million years ago.

Unique features

Unlike other mammals, monotremes have several features that closely resemble those of their reptile ancestors. They have reptilelike bones in their shoulders and lay soft-shelled eggs. Their snouts are uniquely shaped and are used to search for food. Adult monotremes lack teeth and grind their food using bony plates or spines in their mouths.

Monotremes have **unique snouts**. The platypus has a flattened bill, while the echidnas have tubelike beaks.

Reproduction

Female monotremes lay their eggs about three weeks after mating. The duck-billed platypus lays up to three eggs in a burrow, while an echidna egg develops in a temporary pouch on the mother's body.

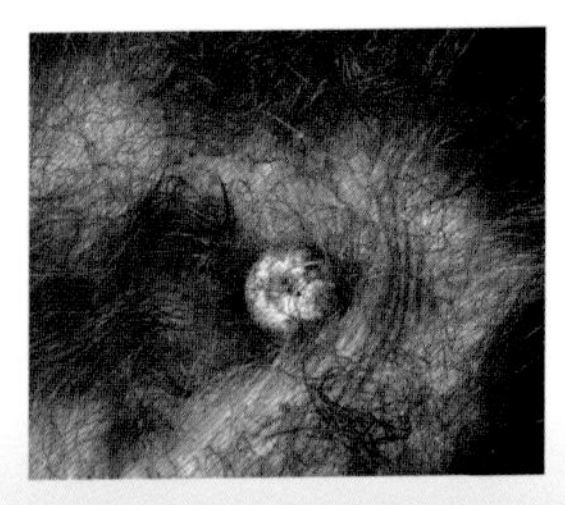

The small and leathery echidna egg is stored and develops in a pouch on the female's belly.

FINDING FOOD

Monotremes find their food in various ways. The short-beaked echidna pokes its tubelike snout in the ground to search for prey and digs out its food with its claws. It catches ants and termites using its long tongue, which is coated with sticky saliva.

Duck-billed platypus

Monotremes have **short limbs**. They move like crocodiles because their limbs are held out at the sides of their bodies rather than below them, as in most other mammals.

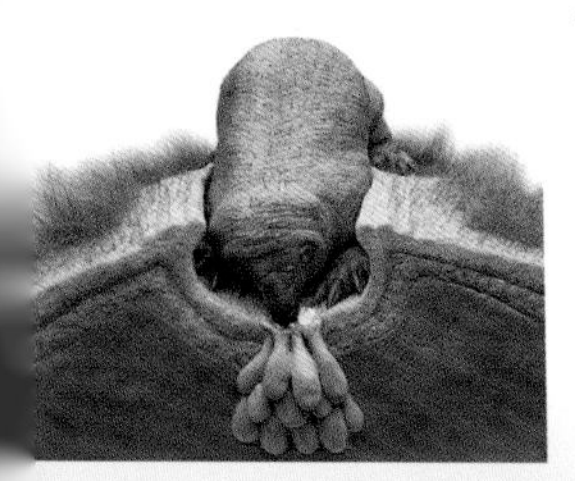

The young hatches out of the egg after 10 days. It continues living in the pouch and laps milk from special patches.

The baby leaves the pouch after 55 days and starts living in the burrow. The mother looks after it for about seven months.

Monotremes

This small group of mammals includes just five species—the duck-billed platypus and four species of echidna—that make up the order Monotremata. Like reptiles, monotremes lay soft-shelled eggs, making these animals unique among mammals.

Short-beaked echidna

Tachyglossus aculeatus

Long, sharp spines cover the head, back, and tail of the short-beaked echidna. When threatened, this animal rolls into a ball, leaving just the tops of its spines exposed. This protects it from most predators.

SIZE 12–18 in (30–45 cm) long

DIET Ants, termites, grubs, and worms

HABITAT Forests, deserts, and savanna

DISTRIBUTION Australia and New Guinea

The animal's pointed spines give it the name "spiny anteater"

Eastern long-beaked echidna

Zaglossus bartoni

ENDANGERED

The eastern long-beaked echidna has a distinctive snout that may be longer than 8 in (20 cm). Its tiny mouth is located at the tip of the snout. It lacks teeth and uses spines on the roof of its mouth and the back of its tongue to mash prey before swallowing.

SIZE 23½–39 in (60–100 cm) long

DIET Earthworms

HABITAT Mountains, forests, and grasslands

DISTRIBUTION New Guinea

Duck-billed platypus

Ornithorhynchus anatinus

Unlike most other mammals, the male platypus is venomous. Its hind leg has a sharp spur, which contains poison glands. The platypus uses this weapon to defend itself and fight rival males during the breeding season.

SIZE 16–23½ in (40–60 cm) long

DIET Crustaceans, worms, and mollusks

HABITAT Wetlands, rivers, and streams

DISTRIBUTION Eastern Australia and Tasmania

Ducklike bill

Spur

Pouched mammals

Kangaroos are pouched mammals. All pouched mammals give birth to live young, which are born at an early stage of development and complete their growth in a pouch, nourished by their mother's milk. The pouch is called the marsupium, and so these mammals are also called marsupials.

GREEN RINGTAIL POSSUM
Most marsupials live in Australia, New Guinea, and nearby islands. This possum lives in northeastern Australia.

Pouched mammals

This diverse set of mammals includes more than 300 species, including bandicoots, kangaroos, opossums, and koalas. They are mainly found in Australia, New Zealand, New Guinea, and South America. Only the Virginia opossum is also found in North America.

What are pouched mammals?

Pouched mammals, or marsupials, give birth to live young at a very early stage of development. In the case of most marsupials, the immature young complete their development in the pouch, nourished by their mother's milk.

Unlike most marsupials, **South American opossums** do not have a pouch. Their young attach themselves to teats on the mother's belly.

A **baby kangaroo**, also called a joey, starts peeking out of its mother's pouch a few months after its birth. At around six months, it starts spending more time outside the pouch.

Reproduction

Marsupials are born with well-developed forelimbs and use these to crawl to their mother's pouch after they are born. They have well-developed nostrils and find the teat using their sense of smell.

A blind and furless baby wallaby begins crawling from the birth opening to its mother's pouch.

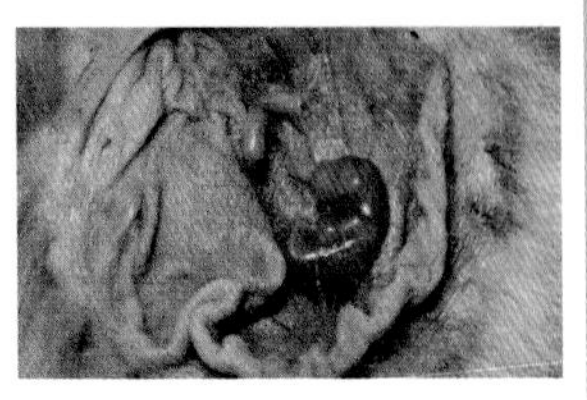

On reaching the pouch, the baby attaches itself to a teat and feeds on its mother's milk.

AUSTRALIAN MAMMALS

Pouched mammals migrated over land from the Americas to Australia millions of years ago when the continents were joined. When Australia broke away from the other continents, these mammals became isolated and started evolving independently.

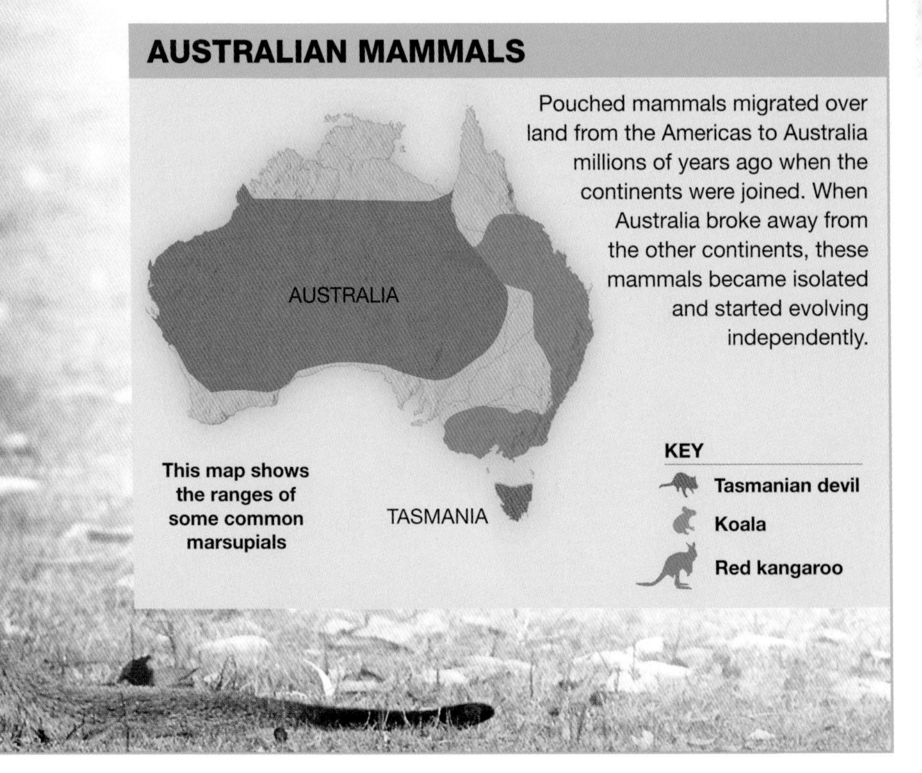

This map shows the ranges of some common marsupials

Opossums

About 90 species of opossum form the order Didelphimorphia. They are also called American opossums because they are all found in the Americas. These small to medium-sized marsupials have long snouts, short limbs, and a long and scaly tail.

Common mouse opossum

Marmosa murina

The common mouse opossum has a very long tail—it is longer than the animal's body and measures between 5–8 in (13.5–21 cm) in length. Its tail can curl around objects and grip them tightly, helping the opossum to climb and carry materials for its nest.

SIZE 4½–5¾ in (11–14.5 cm) long

DIET Insects, small reptiles, birds, and fruit

HABITAT Tropical forests

DISTRIBUTION South America

Babies stay attached to mother's body

The common mouse opossum freezes if startled and won't move even if it is touched.

Virginia opossum

Didelphis virginiana

The Virginia opossum pretends to be dead in order to escape predators and is well-known for this defense tactic. It lies on one side with its eyes and mouth open. Most predators eat live prey so leave the "dead" opossum alone.

SIZE 13–20 in (33–50 cm) long

DIET Fruit, insects, and carrion

HABITAT Forests, woodlands, grasslands, and human settlements

DISTRIBUTION North America and Central America

Water opossum

Chironectes minimus

This opossum is the only marsupial that spends most of its time in water. It swims easily using its webbed hind feet and has dense fur that repels water.

SIZE 10–16 in (26–40 cm) long

DIET Fish, frogs, crabs, and insects

HABITAT Rivers and streams

DISTRIBUTION Central America and South America

Gray four-eyed opossum

Philander opossum

The white spots on this opossum's forehead make it look as if it has four eyes. These eye spots may help in scaring away predators.

SIZE 10–14 in (25–35 cm) long

DIET Leaves, fruit, birds, and worms

HABITAT Tropical forests

DISTRIBUTION Central America and South America

Carnivorous marsupials

These animals have strong jaws, well-developed canine teeth, and sharp claws, except on the big toe. There are about 70 species, which make up the order Dasyuromorphia. They are found mostly in Australia.

Numbat

Myrmecobius fasciatus

The numbat mostly feeds on termites and uses its powerful front feet and large claws to rip open termite nests. It then licks up the termites using its long tongue, which measures up to 4 in (10 cm) in length.

SIZE 8–11 in (20–28 cm) long

DIET Termites

HABITAT Temperate forests

DISTRIBUTION Australia

Eastern quoll

Dasyurus viverrinus

Eastern quolls breed during early winter. The females give birth to a large litter of up to 24 babies, but each female only has six nipples in her pouch. The few young that attach themselves to these and feed manage to survive, while the rest die.

SIZE 11–18 in (28–45 cm) long

DIET Mainly small mammals

HABITAT Forests, woodlands, grasslands, and farmlands

DISTRIBUTION Tasmania

ENDANGERED

Fat-tailed dunnart

Sminthopsis crassicaudata

When food is scarce, fat-tailed dunnarts huddle together to keep warm and save energy. This allows them to survive on a quarter of the food and water they normally need.

SIZE 2½–3½ in (6–9 cm) long

DIET Grubs, worms, and other invertebrates

HABITAT Deserts, grasslands, and woodlands

DISTRIBUTION Australia

Tasmanian devil

Sarcophilus harrisii

ENDANGERED

Tasmanian devils often feed together on a large carcass, ripping the skin and crushing the bones of the dead animal with their powerful jaws. They growl and snarl at each other while feeding on the meat, but do not attack one another.

SIZE 20½–31½ in (52–80 cm) long

DIET Small mammals, birds, and carrion

HABITAT Forests, woodlands, and farmlands

DISTRIBUTION Tasmania

Bandicoots, bilbies, and marsupial moles

The order Peramelemorphia consists of 21 species of bandicoot and bilby. The unrelated order Notoryctemorphia includes two species of marsupial mole. Marsupials in both groups are well adapted to finding invertebrates in the soil.

Southern marsupial mole

Notoryctes typhlops

This marsupial mole moves quickly through light sand in search of food. It lacks external ears and eyes, so it uses its senses of smell and touch to catch its prey.

SIZE 4¾–7 in (12–18 cm) long

DIET Worms, grubs, centipedes, and small reptiles

HABITAT Deserts and grasslands

DISTRIBUTION Australia

Greater bilby

Macrotis lagotis

The greater bilby has a keen sense of hearing. Its enormous ears also help to regulate its body temperature by radiating body heat. This desert-dwelling animal does not drink because it gets all the moisture it needs from the food it eats.

SIZE 12–21½ in (30–55 cm) long

DIET Insects, fruit, and fungi

HABITAT Deserts and grasslands

DISTRIBUTION Australia

New Guinea spiny bandicoot
Echymipera kalubu

These small marsupials live alone and only come together briefly for mating. Highly aggressive and territorial, spiny bandicoots get into regular fights with each other when one enters the territory of another.

SIZE 8–20 in (20–50 cm) long

DIET Insects, worms, and fruit

HABITAT Tropical forests

DISTRIBUTION New Guinea

Long-nosed bandicoot
Perameles nasuta

The long-nosed bandicoot searches for food on the ground. It digs in the ground using its sharp claws and pokes its narrow snout into the soil to reach its prey.

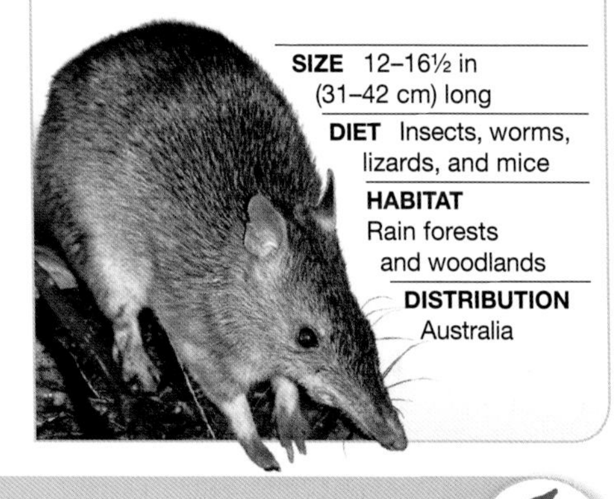

SIZE 12–16½ in (31–42 cm) long

DIET Insects, worms, lizards, and mice

HABITAT Rain forests and woodlands

DISTRIBUTION Australia

Eastern barred bandicoot
Perameles gunnii

Eastern barred bandicoots have one of the shortest pregnancies among mammals—the young are born after just 12 days. They then grow rapidly and leave their mothers' pouches within 60 days.

SIZE 10½–14 in (27–35 cm) long

DIET Mainly invertebrates such as earthworms

HABITAT Forests, grasslands, and farmlands

DISTRIBUTION Australia

Other marsupials

Diprotodontia is the largest order of marsupial. It includes more than 100 species found in Australasia—the region that includes Australia, New Zealand, New Guinea, and the surrounding islands.

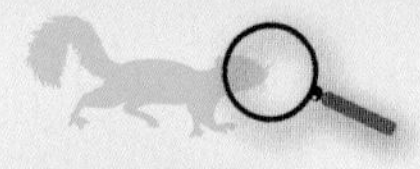

FOCUS ON...
SIZES

Animal size varies tremendously among the marsupials in this order.

▲ The pygmy glider is the world's smallest gliding possum. It is about 5–6 in (13.5–16 cm) long and weighs no more than ½ oz (15 g).

▲ The red kangaroo is the largest marsupial in the world. It can grow to be 6 ft (1.8 m) tall and weigh up to 200 lb (90 kg).

Koala
Phascolarctos cinereus

This bearlike marsupial feeds only on the leaves of the eucalyptus tree. The leaves are highly toxic, but bacteria in the animal's intestines destroy the toxins.

SIZE 25½–32 in (65–82 cm) long

DIET Eucalyptus leaves

HABITAT
Temperate forests

DISTRIBUTION
Eastern Australia

Southern hairy-nosed wombat

Lasiorhinus latifrons

Groups of 5–10 southern hairy-nosed wombats rest together inside burrows that can measure up to 100 ft (30 m) in length. They use their thick-skinned rumps to block the entrance of their burrows against predators.

SIZE 30–37 in (77–95 cm) long

DIET Grass and herbs

HABITAT Grasslands

DISTRIBUTION Southern Australia

Mountain brushtail possum

Trichosurus cunninghami

The mountain brushtail possum has 11 scent-producing glands on its body. It uses its scent to mark its territory and to find mates during the breeding season.

Long tail

SIZE 16–20 in (40–50 cm) long

DIET Fruit, leaves, and flowers

HABITAT Tropical and temperate forests

DISTRIBUTION Southeastern Australia

Sugar glider

Petaurus breviceps

This marsupial glides easily from one tree to another. It has thin flaps of skin that stretch between its forefeet and ankles. These flaps act like a parachute as it glides through the air. The long, bushy tail provides stability and is used for steering the glide.

SIZE 2½–3 in (6.5–8 cm) long

DIET Sap of eucalyptus trees

HABITAT Temperate forests

DISTRIBUTION Australia, Indonesia, and New Guinea

Little pygmy-possum

Cercartetus lepidus

The tail of this little possum is longer than its body. It can support the animal's weight, allowing this possum to hang from bushes and shrubs.

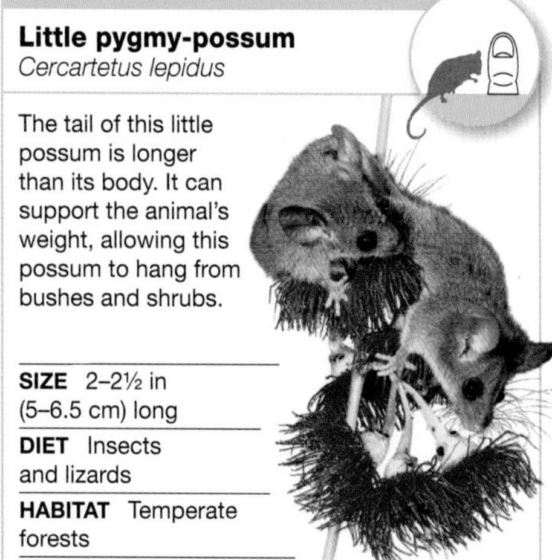

SIZE 2–2½ in (5–6.5 cm) long

DIET Insects and lizards

HABITAT Temperate forests

DISTRIBUTION Australia and Tasmania

Western gray kangaroo

Macropus fuliginosus

Males of this species fight over females. They may also fight rivals for food and resting sites when these are in short supply. They lock arms and try to push each other away, and they may also lean back and kick opponents with their hind feet.

SIZE 3–4½ ft (0.9–1.4 m) long

DIET Grass and leaves

HABITAT Temperate forests and grasslands

DISTRIBUTION Southern Australia

Hind foot

Brush-tailed bettong

Bettongia penicillata

ENDANGERED

The brush-tailed bettong uses its prehensile (grasping) tail to carry material to build its nest. When disturbed, it jumps away at high speed with its head bent downward and its tail held out parallel to the ground.

SIZE 12–15 in (30–38 cm) long

DIET Fungi, roots, bulbs, tubers, and worms

HABITAT Temperate forests

DISTRIBUTION Southwestern Australia

Doria's tree kangaroo
Dendrolagus dorianus

This kangaroo climbs through branches with great care. It uses its short, broad feet and long claws to grip each branch as it climbs, and its tail helps it stay steady.

Despite being the heaviest tree-dwelling marsupial, this kangaroo can jump to a branch 30 ft (9 m) away with ease.

SIZE 20–31 in (51–78 cm) long
DIET Leaves, buds, flowers, and fruit
HABITAT Tropical forests
DISTRIBUTION New Guinea

Musky rat-kangaroo
Hypsiprymnodon moschatus

Unlike most kangaroos that hop using their hind legs, this marsupial bounds on all fours. The grooved soles of its hind feet improve its grip on the ground when running.

SIZE 6–11 in (16–28 cm) long
DIET Fruit, nuts, seeds, and fungi
HABITAT Tropical forests
DISTRIBUTION Australia

Reddish brown fur

Honey possum
Tarsipes rostratus

The lightweight honey possum climbs into flowers to feed on nectar and pollen. It licks off its food using a bristle-tipped tongue, which is 1 in (2.5 cm) long.

SIZE 2½–3½ in (6.5–9 cm) long
DIET Pollen and nectar
HABITAT Temperate forests
DISTRIBUTION Australia

Koalas can sleep for up to

21 hours

each day

CAPTIVE KOALAS

In the wild, koalas usually live on their own and an individual koala's "home" ranges across many eucalyptus trees. Two individuals may meet where their homes overlap. In captivity, however, they are sometimes kept together in groups.

Placental mammals

These mammals evolved around 125 million years ago and are now found worldwide. They form the largest group of mammals. Placental mammals, such as this black panther, give birth to live young. The young develop inside the mother's body, where they are nourished through an organ called the placenta.

LIVING IN WATER
Placental mammals are found in a variety of habitats. Dolphins are well adapted to an aquatic life and even give birth to their young underwater.

Placental mammals

About 5,200 species, including whales, elephants, dogs, and humans, make up this group of mammals. Placental mammals grow inside their mother's womb for a certain period of time (gestation) before being born.

Placenta

Model of a baby gorilla within the uterus of an adult female

What is a placenta?

The placenta is a temporary organ that develops within the walls of the womb. It supplies the growing young with nourishment and oxygen from the mother's body.

LITTER SIZES

A group of young born to a female mammal at one time is called a litter. Litter size varies among mammals. Larger species, such as horses, have long gestation periods and give birth to just one or two young. Smaller mammals, such as dogs, can give birth to up to 10 young at a time.

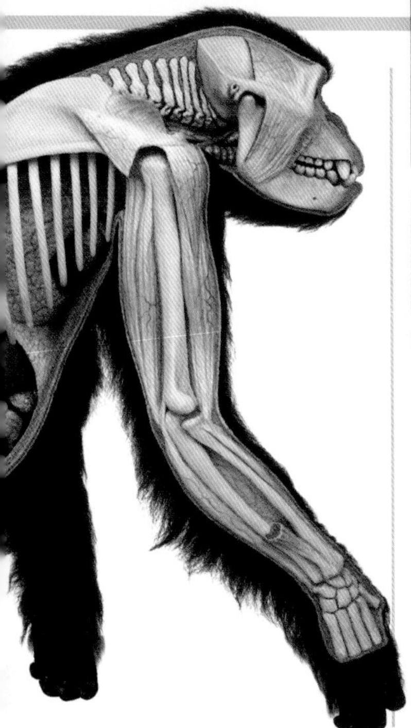

Social groups

Placental mammals form different kinds of social groups. Some live in family groups made up of a male, female, and their most recent offspring. Others, such as baboons, form larger groups that are dominated by a male or a female, while some live alone and only come together for mating.

Reproduction

Although placental mammals are well-developed when they are born, some are more fully formed than others. While large mammals can begin walking within an hour of birth, smaller mammals are born helpless—they grow fur and acquire vision and hearing after birth.

Newborn horses can stand on their feet and suckle milk soon after birth.

Newborn rodents cannot see, hear, or stand and are totally dependent on their mother.

Sengis, golden moles, and tenrecs

Sengis number around 15 species and form the order Macroscelidea. Some 53 species of golden mole and tenrec form the order Afrosoricida. These mammals are found only in Africa and Madagascar.

Gray-faced sengi

Rhynchocyon udzungwensis

Sengis are found in a wide range of habitats from forests to savanna to deserts. In 2005, scientists discovered this species of sengi on the Udzungwa Mountains, Tanzania—the only place it is known to live. It is larger than other species of sengi and can be identified by its colorful fur and gray face.

SIZE 12–12½ in (30–32 cm) long

DIET Mainly insects

HABITAT Tropical forests and mountains

DISTRIBUTION East Africa

Greater hedgehog tenrec

Setifer setosus

White-tipped spines and coarse hair on the body of a tenrec make it resemble a hedgehog. Like a hedgehog, it rolls itself into a prickly ball when it senses danger. A tenrec stays active during the day, however, unlike hedgehogs, which are nocturnal.

SIZE 6–8½ in (15–22 cm) long

DIET Invertebrates, small reptiles, and fruit

HABITAT Tropical forests and grasslands

DISTRIBUTION Madagascar

Juliana's golden mole

Neamblysomus julianae

ENDANGERED

All golden moles are burrowers. The Juliana's golden mole lives underground and pushes its way through loose sandy soil by paddling forward rather than tunneling.

SIZE 4–5 in (10–13 cm) long

DIET Insects, earthworms, and snails

HABITAT Highlands covered in dry grass

DISTRIBUTION South Africa

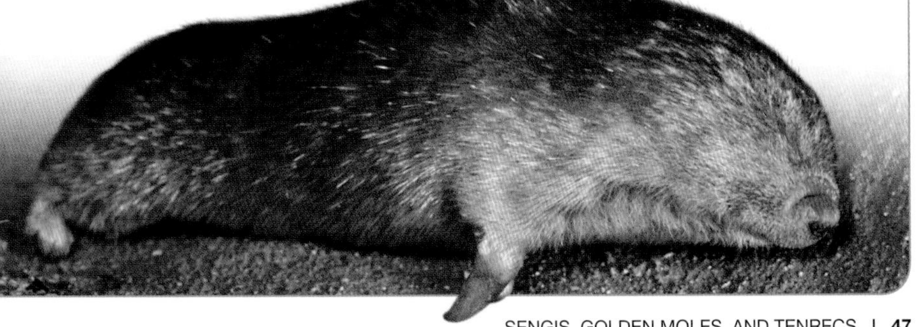

Aardvarks and hyraxes

The piglike aardvark is the only member of the order Tubulidentata. Adult aardvarks have cheek teeth that grow constantly as they are worn down. The rabbitlike hyraxes belong to the unrelated order Hyracoidea, which contains four species.

Aardvark
Orycteropus afer

The aardvark is a powerful digger. It uses its strong claws to dig burrows up to 33 ft (10 m) long. Dense hairs near its nostrils help in filtering out dust particles, while it uses its long tongue to lap up ants and termites from the soil.

Large claws on foot

Rock hyrax
Procavia capensis

Usually found in colonies of about four to 40 individuals, this species is highly social. A colony is headed by a male who guards the group and makes a unique songlike call to warn its members of any impending danger.

SIZE 12–23 in (30–58 cm) long

DIET Leaves, wood, bark, and stems

HABITAT Mountains, grasslands, and deserts

DISTRIBUTION Africa and western Asia

SIZE 5¼ ft (1.6 m) long

DIET Ants and termites

HABITAT Grasslands and savanna

DISTRIBUTION Sub-Saharan Africa

An aardvark's hind feet have five toes each, while its forefeet have only four each.

Bush hyrax

Heterohyrax brucei

This mammal is adapted to its rocky habitat. Soft pads on its feet are moistened by fluids from glands. These pads act as cushions for the bush hyrax's feet and help the animal to move around easily on rocky terrain.

SIZE 12–15 in (30–38 cm) long

DIET Mainly grass and fruits

HABITAT Rocky areas

DISTRIBUTION Africa

Dugongs and manatees

These plant-eating marine mammals belong to the order Sirenia, which includes the dugong and three species of manatee. They swim to the water surface to breathe, but can remain submerged in shallow water for up to 20 minutes at a time. Fewer than 150,000 of these mammals are left today.

Dugong

Dugong dugon

Also known as the "sea cow," a dugong has a chubby, cowlike body and spends a lot of time grazing on the grass and plants that grow on the seabed. The dugong's eyesight is poor and it uses the long whiskers on its snout to find its food.

SIZE 8¼–13 ft (2.5–4 m) long

DIET Sea grass, roots, and leaves

HABITAT Rivers, streams, and coastal areas

DISTRIBUTION East Africa, southern and Southeast Asia, northern Australia, and Pacific Islands

Seafarers in the 17th century mistook dugongs for the mythical creatures known as mermaids.

West Indian manatee

Trichechus manatus

Like the dugong, the manatee also spends hours grazing on sea grass. It can hold food with its flippers (paddle-shaped limbs) and uses its flexible upper lip to direct food into its mouth. These creatures gather in groups of 2–20 when food is plentiful.

SIZE 8¼–14¾ ft (2.5–4.5 m) long

DIET Sea grass, roots, and leaves

HABITAT Rivers, streams, and coastal areas

DISTRIBUTION Southeastern US, northern South America, and the Caribbean

Amazonian manatee

Trichechus inunguis

Manatees lack hind limbs. They steer through water using their flippers and strong, flat tail. This particular species can only be found in the waters of the Amazon River and its tributaries.

SIZE 6½–9 ft (2–2.8 m) long

DIET Sea grass, roots, and leaves

HABITAT Rivers, streams, and ponds

DISTRIBUTION South America

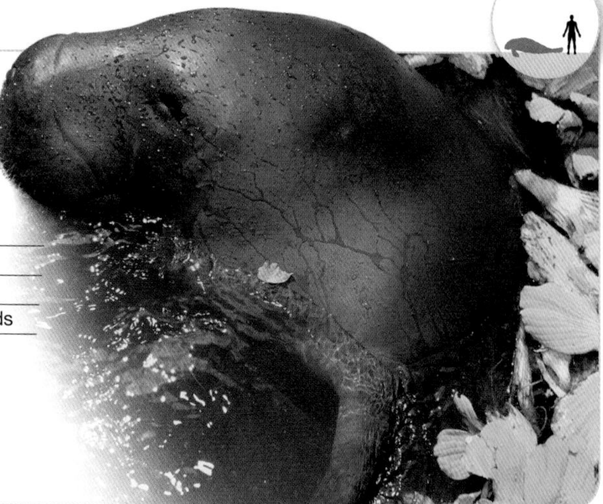

Elephants

The largest animals on land, elephants can weigh more than 13,000 lb (6,000 kg). They have large, fan-shaped ears, long incisor teeth called tusks, and a flexible trunk. Three species of elephant make up the order Proboscidea.

FOCUS ON...
MOLAR TEETH

The molar teeth of African elephants are different from those of the Asiatic elephant.

◀ An African elephant has fewer ridges on its molar teeth. These ridges are shaped like diamonds.

◀ The Asiatic elephant eats more grass than African elephants and has a greater number of ridges on its molar teeth. The ridges lie parallel to one another.

Asiatic elephant
Elephas maximus

ENDANGERED

An Asiatic elephant has one fingerlike structure at the tip of its trunk, while its African cousins have a pair. This structure helps it to grasp small objects with its trunk.

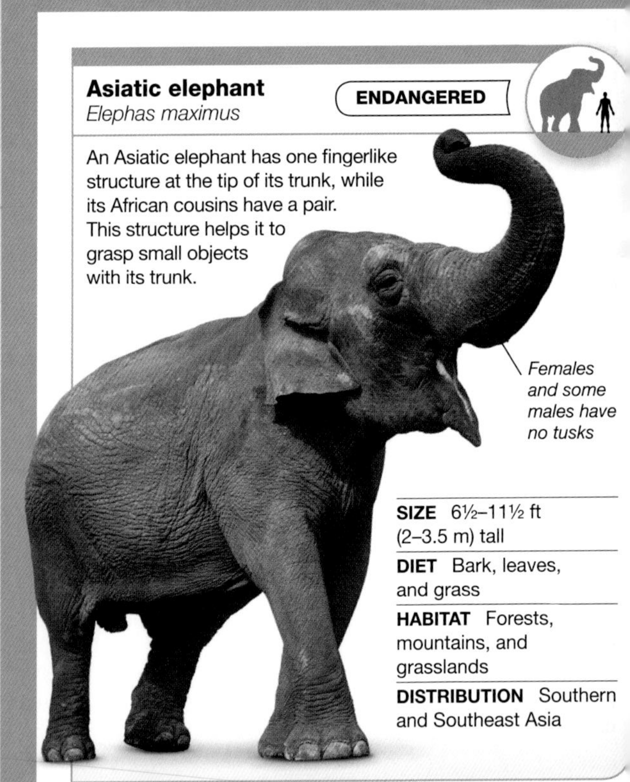

Females and some males have no tusks

SIZE 6½–11½ ft (2–3.5 m) tall

DIET Bark, leaves, and grass

HABITAT Forests, mountains, and grasslands

DISTRIBUTION Southern and Southeast Asia

African savanna elephant
Loxodonta africana

These elephants sometimes charge at predators, especially when defending a mother elephant and her baby. They charge with their heads lowered slightly before trumpeting.

SIZE 13–16½ ft (4–5 m) tall

DIET Bark, leaves, and grass

HABITAT Grasslands, savanna, deserts, and rain forests

DISTRIBUTION Africa

African forest elephant
Loxodonta cyclotis

ENDANGERED

In addition to being smaller than the African savanna elephant, this species has more rounded ears and a hairier trunk. Its tusks point downward and this helps it to move easily through its dense forest habitat.

SIZE 10–13 ft (3–4 m) tall

DIET Bark, leaves, branches, grass, and fruit

HABITAT Tropical forests and mountains

DISTRIBUTION West and central Africa

An elephant's
trunk has
more than

40,000 muscles

but no bones

ELEPHANT HERD
Elephants live in herds made up of females and their infants. The oldest female is the leader of the group. Males leave their herd once they become adults and form smaller groups. During a drought, elephant herds gather near available sources of water.

Armadillos

An armorlike, hardened skin protects most of the body of an armadillo. About 21 species of armadillo form the order Cingulata. These mammals dig into the ground with their strong forelegs. They mainly eat insects, which they lap up with their tongues.

Giant armadillo

Priodontes maximus

The giant armadillo uses the large claws on its forefeet to rip open termite and ant mounds and feed on the insects living inside. It also uses its claws to dig burrows for shelter during the day.

SIZE 29½–39 in (75–100 cm) long

DIET Termites, ants, snakes, and lizards

HABITAT Grasslands and forests

DISTRIBUTION Northern and central South America

Six-banded armadillo

Euphractus sexcinctus

This armadillo's shell has between six to eight bands covered in hard keratin—the same substance found in horns. Although it is unable to curl into a ball like some other species, the soft skin between its bands make its shell flexible.

SIZE 16–19½ in (40–49 cm) long

DIET Insects, fruit, tubers, nuts, and carrion

HABITAT Grasslands, savanna, and forests

DISTRIBUTION South America

Northern naked-tailed armadillo

Cabassous centralis

Unlike other armadillos, this species lacks a hard shell on its tail. When threatened by predators, it digs into the ground so that only its top body armor is exposed.

SIZE 12–16 in (30–40 cm) long

DIET Ants and termites

HABITAT Savanna and forests

DISTRIBUTION Central America and northern South America

Big hairy armadillo

Chaetophractus villosus

This armadillo burrows under or into animal carcasses and feeds on the maggots (fly larvae) that are found in the rotting remains.

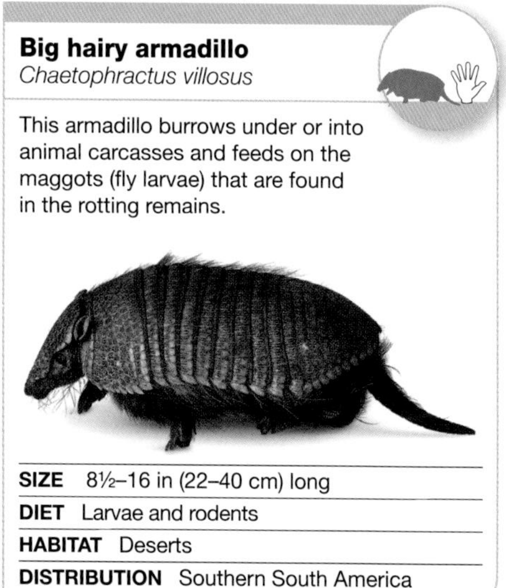

SIZE 8½–16 in (22–40 cm) long

DIET Larvae and rodents

HABITAT Deserts

DISTRIBUTION Southern South America

Sloths and anteaters

Although they look different from one another, both sloths and anteaters have coarse coats and fewer teeth than other mammals. The anteaters are toothless, while the sloths have peglike cheek teeth. Eleven species form the order Pilosa.

Linnaeus' two-toed sloth

Choloepus didactylus

Silky anteater

Cyclopes didactylus

This anteater tends to live in silk-cotton trees. The fibers covering the seedpods on these trees look similar to its fur, and this helps in camouflaging the animal from predators.

SIZE 6–8 in (16–21 cm) long

DIET Mainly ants

HABITAT Tropical forests

DISTRIBUTION Central America to northern South America

Giant anteater

Myrmecophaga tridactyla

The giant anteater rips open ant nests and termite mounds with its large front feet. It then scoops up its prey using its long tongue, which is covered with sticky saliva.

The Linnaeus' two-toed sloth spends its time traveling from tree to tree in search of food. Sloths are the slowest mammals and this species can take an entire day to move from one tree to another.

SIZE 18–34 in (46–86 cm) long

DIET Leaves and fruit

HABITAT Rain forests

DISTRIBUTION Northern South America

SIZE 3¼–6½ ft (1–2 m) long

DIET Ants, termites, and other insects

HABITAT Tropical forests and grasslands

DISTRIBUTION Central America to South America

Pale-throated sloth

Bradypus tridactylus

Using its hooklike claws, the pale-throated sloth can hang from branches for as long as 18 hours. It may even fall asleep in this position.

SIZE 18–30 in (45–76 cm) long

DIET Twigs, buds, and leaves

HABITAT Rain forests

DISTRIBUTION South America

Long, shaggy fur

Rabbits, hares, and pikas

The order Lagomorpha includes about 92 species of rabbit, hare, and pika. These plant-eating mammals spend much of their time gnawing on food. Their eyes are located on the sides of their head. This gives them an all-around view—a feature that is useful for spotting predators easily.

American pika

Ochotona princeps

Pikas save food to survive the harsh winter. They collect plants that rot slowly and store them just outside their dens. These stored plants become a ready source of food during the winter when snow covers the ground.

SIZE 6–8½ in (16–22 cm) long

DIET Grass, herbs, and flowers

HABITAT Mountains

DISTRIBUTION North America

Arctic hare

Lepus arcticus

The Arctic hare's winter coat is almost pure white and camouflages the animal in the snow. In the summer, however, its coat usually turns gray-brown.

SIZE 17–26 in (43–66 cm) long

DIET Grass, herbs, and shrubs

HABITAT Northern polar regions

DISTRIBUTION Northern Canada and Greenland

Cream Angora rabbit

Oryctolagus cuniculus

The Angora rabbit is prized for its fur, which is used to produce the softest wool. The fur on its back and upper body is usually the longest and cleanest and is used to make the wool.

SIZE 10–15 in (25–38 cm) long

DIET Grass, herbs, and leaves

HABITAT Human settlements

DISTRIBUTION Originated in Turkey

Black-tailed jackrabbit

Lepus californicus

The huge ears of the black-tailed jackrabbit can measure up to 6 in (15 cm) in length. They help the animal to hear even the faintest sounds made by predators.

SIZE 18½–25 in (47–63 cm) long

DIET Mainly grass

HABITAT Deserts and grasslands

DISTRIBUTION Southwestern and central US

Pygmy rabbit

Brachylagus idahoensis

These tiny rabbits live in areas covered by sagebrush, a type of bushy shrub. The plant forms a major part of their diet and also shelters them from predators. Quite often the rabbits make their burrows just under these shrubs.

SIZE 8½–11½ in (22–29 cm) long

DIET Mainly sagebrush

HABITAT Deserts

DISTRIBUTION Western North America

Rodents

This large group of mammals includes more than 2,000 species that make up the order Rodentia. Rodents have a pair of incisors in both the upper and lower jaws. The large upper incisors are kept sharp by constant gnawing.

FOCUS ON...
PROBLEMS
Rodents cause a number of problems for humans.

▲ The house mouse is a household pest. It chews up electrical wiring and items such as furniture and books.

▲ Brown rats are farmland pests that eat and spoil crops and stored grains.

▲ Rat fleas, carried by the black rat, spread a deadly infection called plague.

Eurasian red squirrel
Scuirus vulgaris

The Eurasian red squirrel has a distinctive tail that measures 6–8 in (15–20 cm) in length. It jumps from one tree to the next using its tail to balance and steer itself. When sleeping in its nest (drey), the squirrel curls its tail around its body to keep itself warm.

SIZE 8–10 in (20–25 cm) long

DIET Mainly seeds, fungi, and shoots

HABITAT Temperate forests, coniferous forests, and mountains

DISTRIBUTION Europe and Asia

Southern flying squirrel

Glaucomys volans

Flying squirrels leap from a height and use the parachutelike, furry membrane between their front and hind legs to glide from one tree to another. Their long tails help to steer the glide.

SIZE 5–6 in (13–15 cm) long

DIET Leaves, fruit, grains, nuts, birds' eggs, and carrion

HABITAT Temperate forests

DISTRIBUTION Eastern US

Gliding membrane

Black-tailed prairie dog

Cynomys ludovicianus

These rodents live in extensive burrow systems called towns. The burrows are usually located between 6½–10 ft (2–3 m) below the ground and can be up to 33 ft (10 m) long.

SIZE 11–12 in (28–30 cm) long

DIET Leaves, stems, and roots

HABITAT Grasslands

DISTRIBUTION North America

Edible dormouse

Glis glis

Ancient Romans captured and ate these rodents. This practice inspired the animal's name. The edible dormouse has been traditionally hunted and eaten in Slovenia for hundreds of years.

SIZE 5–8 in (13–20 cm) long

DIET Leaves, grains, seeds, nuts, fruit, birds, and insects

HABITAT Temperate forests

DISTRIBUTION Europe and western Asia

Golden hamster

Mesocricetus auratus

Most of the hamsters that are kept as pets today are the descendants of a single female captured in 1930. The original pet hamsters were short-haired, but a long-haired variety and several different colors have since been developed.

SIZE 5–5¼ in (13–13.5 cm) long

DIET Seeds, nuts, and insects

HABITAT Grasslands and human settlements

DISTRIBUTION Originated in western Asia

Merriam's kangaroo rat

Dipodomys merriami

Like a kangaroo, this small placental mammal usually hops from one place to another on its hind feet. Its long tail balances the animal as it bounds around.

SIZE 3–5½ in (8–14 cm) long

DIET Mainly seeds

HABITAT Deserts and grasslands

DISTRIBUTION Southwestern US and Mexico

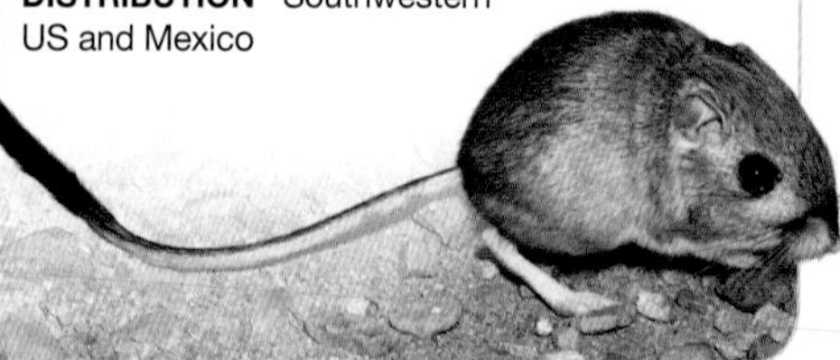

Norway lemming

Lemmus lemmus

The population of this species rises sharply every 3–4 years, if plenty of food is available. During such periods, a pair of Norway lemmings can produce more than 100 offspring within a span of six months. The animals soon consume all the food in their surroundings and migrate in search of more food.

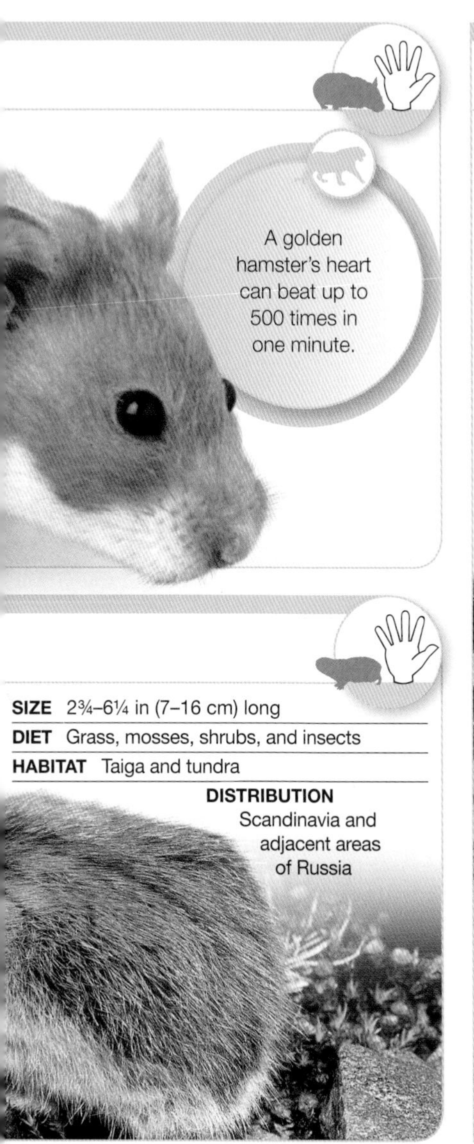

SIZE 2¾–6¼ in (7–16 cm) long

DIET Grass, mosses, shrubs, and insects

HABITAT Taiga and tundra

DISTRIBUTION Scandinavia and adjacent areas of Russia

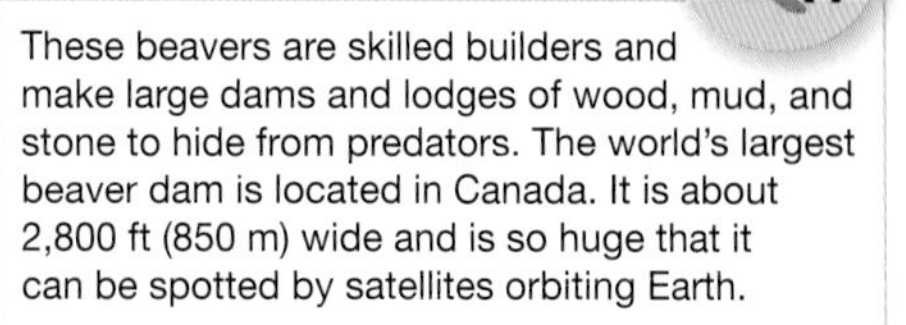

American beaver

Castor canadensis

These beavers are skilled builders and make large dams and lodges of wood, mud, and stone to hide from predators. The world's largest beaver dam is located in Canada. It is about 2,800 ft (850 m) wide and is so huge that it can be spotted by satellites orbiting Earth.

SIZE 29–34½ in (74–88 cm) long

DIET Leaves, shoots, twigs, and bark

HABITAT Wetlands, rivers, and streams

DISTRIBUTION North America

Brown rat

Rattus norvegicus

This nocturnal hunter uses its keen sense of smell to find food as far as 1.8 miles (3 km) away. Packs of up to 200 rats, dominated by large males, are known to prey on animals as large as rabbits and poultry.

SIZE 8–11 in (20–28 cm) long

DIET Plant matter, small mammals, small reptiles, birds, fish, eggs, carrion, insects, and worms

HABITAT Grasslands, rivers, streams, wetlands, and human settlements

DISTRIBUTION Worldwide except polar regions

Capybara

Hydrochoerus hydrochaeris

The word *capybara* means "master of grasses" in Guaraní, a language used by the Tupí-Guaraní tribe in South America. True to its name, the capybara spends most of its time feeding on grasses and other vegetation.

SIZE 3½–4¼ ft (1.1–1.3 m) long

DIET Mainly grass and aquatic plants

HABITAT Grasslands, wetlands, rivers, and streams

DISTRIBUTION South America

Chinchilla

Chinchilla lanigera

Prized for its soft, silky fur, the chinchilla has been hunted by humans for many years. It is named after a South American tribe called Chincha, the members of which used to wear clothes made from the rodent's velvetlike fur.

Crested porcupine

Hystrix cristata

A porcupine's spines are modified hairs made up of a substance called keratin, which is also found in horns and nails. Crested porcupines rattle their quills (spines) when threatened and, if that does not scare off a predator, they will run backward and jab their spines into the hunter.

SIZE 23½–40 in (60–100 cm) long

DIET Fruit and carrion

HABITAT Savanna, grasslands, forests, and rocky terrain

DISTRIBUTION Northern Africa and sub-Saharan Africa

SIZE 8½–9 in (22–23 cm) long

DIET Grass and leaves

HABITAT Mountains

DISTRIBUTION South America

Naked mole rat

Heterocephalus glaber

Naked mole rats form large colonies and have a unique social system among rodents in which only the dominant female produces pups. Other females in the colony look after the babies.

SIZE 3–3½ in (8–9 cm) long

DIET Roots, bulbs, tubers, and underground parts of plants

HABITAT Deserts

DISTRIBUTION East Africa

EASTERN GRAY SQUIRREL

Every fall the eastern gray squirrel gathers nuts and seeds so that it has enough food to survive the winter. It hides its food in hundreds of different places. An excellent memory helps it to remember the locations of many hidden stores of food.

Squirrels can

rotate their hind feet

backward for better grip when climbing down trees headfirst

Tree shrews and flying lemurs

Twenty species of tree shrew form the order Scandentia. They live on trees but spend a lot of time on the ground. The order Dermoptera contains two species of flying lemur, which only glide between trees.

Lesser tree shrew
Tupaia minor

This skilled climber escapes mongooses by running up trees. Its sharp claws improve its grip on branches and its long tail helps it balance.

SIZE 4½–5 in (11.5–13.5 cm) long
DIET Fruit, leaves, seeds, insects, and carrion
HABITAT Tropical forests
DISTRIBUTION Southeast Asia

Greater tree shrew
Tupaia tana

Greater tree shrews spend most of their time on the ground. They climb up trees for short periods of time to scan the area for danger, using their keen senses of hearing, smell, and vision.

Newborn greater tree shrews can sleep for up to 40 hours at a time.

SIZE 6–9 in (15–23 cm) long
DIET Insects, fruit, and leaves
HABITAT Tropical forests
DISTRIBUTION Southeast Asia

Malayan colugo

Cynocephalus variegatus

These flying lemurs have a furry membrane stretching from their necks to the tips of their fingers and even their tails. This membrane spreads out when they splay their limbs during glides from one tree to another. The Malayan colugo is the best glider among mammals. The large surface area of its gliding membrane, when stretched out, allows it to glide up to 330 ft (100 m) between trees without losing too much height.

SIZE 13–16½ in (33–42 cm) long

DIET Young leaves and buds

HABITAT Rain forests and mountains

DISTRIBUTION Southeast Asia

Philippine flying lemur

Cynocephalus volans

Gliding membrane

This mammal is neither a lemur nor does it fly. Instead, it is a glider like the Malayan colugo, and it glides from one tree to another using its gliding membrane. This parachutelike membrane, however, hinders other movements, such as climbing, making the animal labor more over them.

SIZE 13½–16½ in (34–42 cm) long

DIET Leaves, buds, fruit, and flowers

HABITAT Tropical forests

DISTRIBUTION Philippines

Primates

This order is a varied group of mammal, including prosimians, monkeys, and apes. Most primates form complex social groups. They have grasping hands, and some have a prehensile (grasping) tail. About 382 species make up this order.

Crowned sifaka

Propithecus coronatus

The crowned sifaka moves between trees by leaping across distances up to 33 ft (10 m) and clinging to the tree trunk. If the distance between the trees is too great, it moves on the ground on its hind legs by skipping sideways with its arms above its head.

SIZE 15½–18 in (39.5–45.5 cm) long

DIET Leaves, buds, fruit, and flowers

HABITAT Temperate forests and mangroves

DISTRIBUTION Madagascar

The sifaka defines its territory by making "shi-fak" calls that sound like hiccups.

FOCUS ON...

TYPES

Prosimians, monkeys, and apes are the three main kinds of primate.

▲ Lorises, tarsiers, and lemurs, such as this aye-aye, are prosimians. Only some have tails.

▲ The emperor tamarin has a long tail—a trait common to all monkeys, including baboons.

◀ Gorillas, humans, orangutans, chimpanzees, and gibbons, such as this lar gibbon, are apes, which lack a tail.

Slow loris

Nycticebus coucang

Female lorises secrete toxins from glands in their elbows. They mix it with their saliva and apply it on the fur of their young. The toxic fur keeps predators away from the young.

SIZE 10–15 in (26–38 cm) long

DIET Birds, lizards, and fruit

HABITAT Tropical forests

DISTRIBUTION Southeast Asia

Moholi bushbaby

Galago moholi

Bushbabies, or galagos, hunt only during the night. A special layer at the back of their eyes acts like a mirror. It reflects light back into their eyes, giving them a brighter view of their dark surroundings. This makes them excellent nocturnal hunters.

SIZE 6–6½ in (15–17 cm) long

DIET Mainly insects and plant sap

HABITAT Tropical forests

DISTRIBUTION Sub-Saharan Africa

Ring-tailed lemur

Lemur catta

The ring-tailed lemur lives in groups, or troops, of 5–25 animals. The lemurs interact with each other using a variety of calls. Some of these calls are used to communicate within or between troops, and others to raise an alarm if predators are lurking nearby.

SIZE 15–18 in (39–46 cm) long

DIET Flowers, fruit, leaves, and bark

HABITAT Tropical forests

DISTRIBUTION Madagascar

Gray woolly monkey
Lagothrix cana

ENDANGERED

Despite being quite heavy, this monkey can easily jump from one tree to another. Its muscular shoulders and hips help the animal to swing through trees, and its long tail supports its body mainly when feeding and reaching for food. The tail is prehensile and the underside of its tip is hairless, which increases its grip on branches.

SIZE 20–25½ in (50–65 cm) long

DIET Mainly fruit

HABITAT Rain forests

DISTRIBUTION Central South America

Venezuelan red howler
Alouatta seniculus

A chorus of calls made by a group of these monkeys can be heard from more than 1¼ miles (2 km) away. Some calls act as a warning for other animals to stay away from their territory.

SIZE 20–25 in (50–63 cm) long

DIET Leaves, fruit, and flowers

HABITAT Rain forests and coastal areas

DISTRIBUTION Northwestern South America

Black-faced spider monkey
Ateles chamek

The limbs and tail of this monkey are longer than its body, giving it a spiderlike appearance. Its hook-shaped hands lack a well-formed thumb. This primate swings from one tree to another using its flexible limbs. The long tail helps it to balance itself and is most useful when reaching for food.

SIZE 16–20½ in (40–52 cm) long

DIET Fruit, flowers, leaves, grubs, termites, and honey

HABITAT Rain forests

DISTRIBUTION Western South America

White-faced saki

Pithecia pithecia

Male and female white-faced sakis look remarkably different from each other. The male monkeys have black fur with a pale white or gold face, while the females have gray-brown fur with a dark face.

Long, black fur on a male saki

SIZE 13½–14 in (34–35 cm) long

DIET Fruit, nuts, seeds, leaves, and flowers

HABITAT Tropical forests and coastal areas

DISTRIBUTION Northern South America

ENDANGERED

Red bald-headed uakari

Cacajao calvus rubicundus

The bright red face of this monkey may indicate good health. In the breeding season, females select males with the reddest heads.

Long, thick fur

SIZE 15–22½ in (38–57 cm) long

DIET Fruit, insects, frogs, lizards, and bats

HABITAT Rain forests

DISTRIBUTION Northwestern South America

Northern night monkey
Aotus trivirgatus

Also called the owl monkey, this primate is the only monkey that forages for food at night. Its large eyes collect even dim light in its surroundings, helping the animal to locate its food in the dark.

Dark, bushy tail

SIZE 9½–19 in (24–48 cm) long

DIET Mainly fruit and also insects

HABITAT Tropical forests

DISTRIBUTION Northern South America

Weeper capuchin
Cebus olivaceus

The weeper capuchin forms groups of about 30 monkeys. Adult females in each group tend to look after the young together. This group behavior is called "allomothering."

SIZE 14½–18 in (37–46 cm) long

DIET Seeds, fruit, and insects

HABITAT Tropical forests

DISTRIBUTION Northeastern South America

Black-capped squirrel monkey
Saimiri boliviensis

Squirrel monkeys form large troops with up to 200 members. Within a troop, there are smaller groups of adult males and females with their young. If a monkey finds food, other members quickly gather around to take their share.

SIZE 10½–12½ in (27–32 cm) long

DIET Insects and fruit

HABITAT Tropical forests

DISTRIBUTION Western and central South America

Golden lion tamarin
Leontopithecus rosalia

ENDANGERED

This monkey can be identified easily by its silklike, golden fur and gray face. It uses its long, clawed hands to dig out grubs from trees and to hold fruit, which makes up most of its diet.

Scientists have bred golden lion tamarins in captivity, increasing their population from fewer than 300 in 1996, to more than 1,000 today.

SIZE 8–10 in (20–25 cm) long

DIET Fruit, insects, tree gum, and nectar

HABITAT Tropical forests

DISTRIBUTION Rio São João Basin in South America

Pygmy marmoset
Cebuella pygmaea

When it curls up, a pygmy marmoset can fit into a human palm. It is the smallest monkey in the world. It may live for about 12 years in the wild and 20 years in captivity.

SIZE 4¾–6 in (12–15 cm) long

DIET Nectar, fruit, plant sap, and spiders

HABITAT Tropical forests

DISTRIBUTION Western South America

Japanese macaque
Macaca fuscata

Like humans, one population of Japanese macaque have a habit of taking a dip in hot springs to stay warm. Macaques have also been known to wash their food in seawater.

SIZE 18½–23½ in (47–60 cm) long

DIET Fruit, insects, plants, and soil

HABITAT Forests and mountains

DISTRIBUTION Japan

Olive baboon
Papio anubis

This monkey forms closely knit social groups of about 150 adult females, a few males, and their offspring. Once the males mature into adults, they leave the group.

SIZE 23½–34 in (60–86 cm) long

DIET Fruit, leaves, insects, and lizards

HABITAT Tropical forests, savanna, grasslands, and mountains

DISTRIBUTION Sub-Saharan Africa

Siamang
Symphalangus syndactylus

ENDANGERED

The siamang is the largest and loudest of the gibbons. When calling, it inflates a sac in its throat to about the size of a grapefruit to amplify the sound. This loud call warns other animals against entering its territory.

Hooklike hand helps to grab branches easily

Like tightrope walkers, siamangs can walk on branches of tall trees with their arms outstretched.

SIZE 36 in (90 cm) long

DIET Leaves, fruit, and grubs

HABITAT Tropical forests and mountains

DISTRIBUTION Southeast Asia

Mandrill

Mandrillus sphinx

Mandrills usually live in groups of about 20. A dominant male heads each group. The colors on its face are brighter than those on other mandrills in the group. It also has large canine teeth, which it displays if threatened by a predator or approached by rivals.

SIZE 25–32 in (63–81 cm) long

DIET Fruit, seeds, eggs, and small animals

HABITAT Tropical forests

DISTRIBUTION West central Africa

Most vivid scarlet color is seen on dominant male in a group

Five digits on hand

Western gorilla

Gorilla gorilla

ENDANGERED

Gorillas live in troops of five to 10 animals, with many females and one dominant male, called the "silverback" because of the silvery fur on its back. When threatened, the silverback roars and then beats its chest with cupped hands. If this tactic does not work, the massive ape may charge at its attacker.

SIZE 4¼–6¼ ft (1.3–1.9 m) tall

DIET Fruit, leaves, stems, seeds, and termites

HABITAT Tropical forests

DISTRIBUTION Central Africa

Bornean orangutan

Pongo pygmaeus

ENDANGERED

The Bornean orangutan is the largest tree-dwelling animal in the world. It moves with ease from tree to tree using its grasping hands and feet. Its arms are very long and may reach 6½ ft (2 m) or more in length.

SIZE 3½–4½ ft (1.1–1.4 m) tall

DIET Fruit, leaves, seeds, birds' eggs, and insects

HABITAT Tropical forests

DISTRIBUTION Southeast Asia

Common chimpanzee
Pan troglodytes

ENDANGERED

Face lacks fur

Arm is longer than leg

Thumb is opposable, which lets the animal grip precisely

Chimpanzees live in groups of 50 to 150 animals. Smaller groups go out to forage for food, and the males cooperate closely when hunting. Common chimpanzees have been known to hunt with tools—from twigs used to dig out termites to sticks for spearing bushbabies.

SIZE 25–36 in (63–90 cm) tall

DIET Mainly fruit and leaves, but also insects and sometimes other monkeys

HABITAT Tropical forests

DISTRIBUTION West to central Africa

Human
Homo sapiens

Modern humans—*Homo sapiens*—evolved in Africa. They spread out to the rest of the world and had covered Eurasia, Australia, and the Americas about 15,000 years ago. Today, they live on every continent, except Antarctica (although some scientists are temporarily based in research stations there). The human population reached 7 billion in 2012.

SIZE 4–7 ft (1.2–2.1 m) tall

DIET Plant and animal products

HABITAT All habitats except underwater

DISTRIBUTION Worldwide

Nostrils placed closely together

Opposable thumb

Upright stance

Toes help in walking and balance

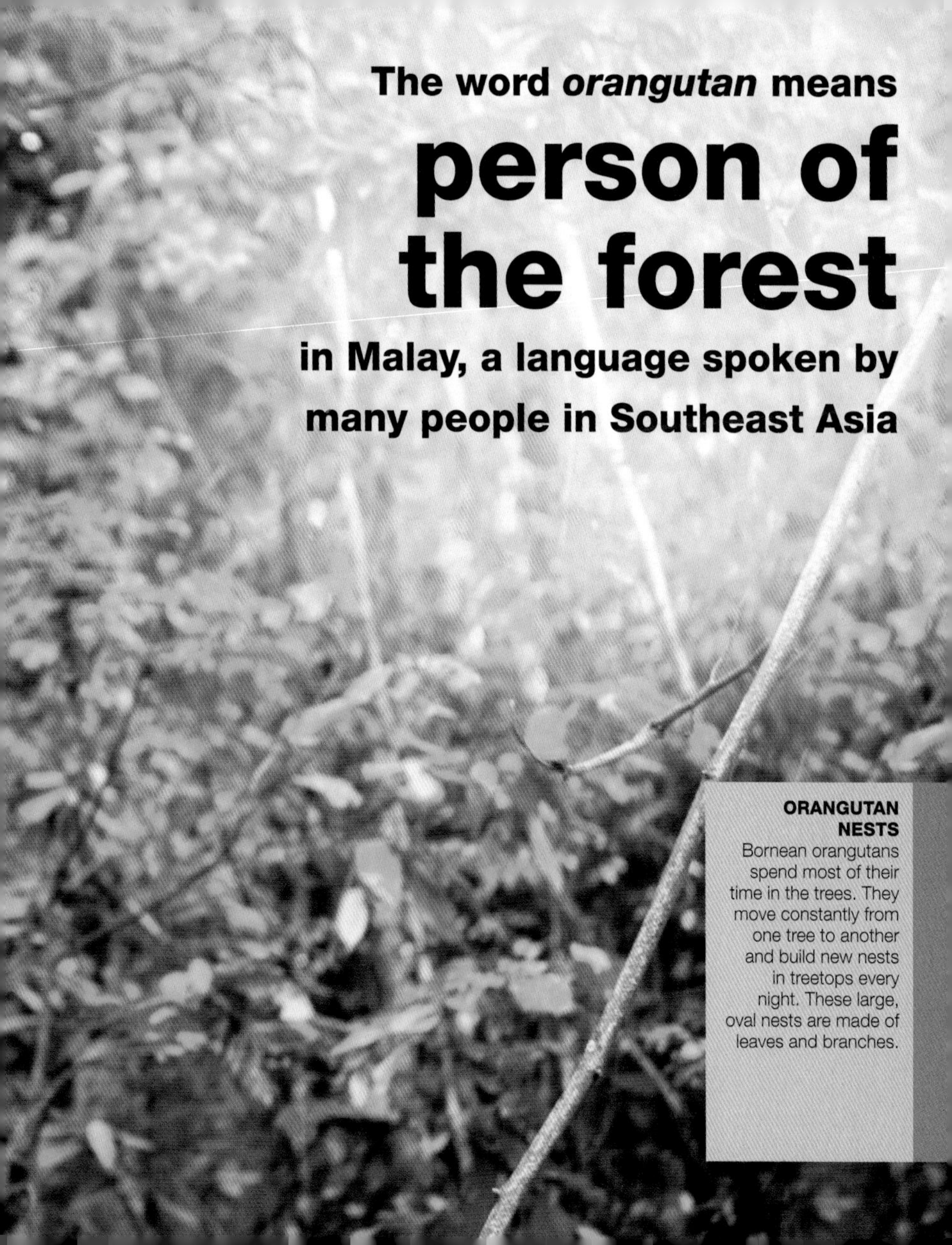

The word *orangutan* means

person of the forest

in Malay, a language spoken by many people in Southeast Asia

ORANGUTAN NESTS

Bornean orangutans spend most of their time in the trees. They move constantly from one tree to another and build new nests in treetops every night. These large, oval nests are made of leaves and branches.

FOCUS ON...
USING SENSES

Bats use various senses to find their food.

▲ All bats have a good sense of smell. Some bats, such as this flying fox, also have large eyes that help them see clearly at night.

▲ Other bats, such as this long-eared bat, have large ears that can pick up even the faintest echoes made by their high-pitched calls.

Bats

Bats are the only mammals capable of flying, not just gliding. They fly using wings made of flaps of skin that extend from the sides of their bodies across their elongated fingers. More than 1,000 species of bat form the order Chiroptera.

Franquet's epauletted bat
Epomops franqueti

Large groups of these bats roost together on trees. The males in these groups make high-pitched whistling calls from the treetops to attract mates. Their collective din is a common sound in African forests.

SIZE 4½–6 in (11–15 cm) long
DIET Fruit and leaves
HABITAT Tropical forests
DISTRIBUTION West and central Africa

Lesser horseshoe bat

Rhinolophus hipposideros

Bats use echolocation to find prey. They make ultrasonic calls—high-pitched chirps that cannot be heard by humans. These chirps reflect off prey, and the echoes allow the bats to locate it. This bat has a distinctive horseshoe-shaped growth on its nose—called a nose-leaf—which helps to amplify its ultrasonic calls.

SIZE 1½ in (4 cm) long

DIET Small flying insects

HABITAT Forests, woodlands, and grasslands

DISTRIBUTION Europe, northern Africa, and western Asia

Ghost bat

Macroderma gigas

This bat is named for its wings, which are almost transparent and make it appear ghostly at night. It swoops down on prey, wrapping its victims in its wings before biting and killing them.

SIZE 4–4¾ in (10–12 cm) long

DIET Insects, birds, lizards, and other bats

HABITAT Tropical forests and savanna

DISTRIBUTION Western and northern Australia

Greater bulldog bat

Noctilio leporinus

The greater bulldog bat hunts close to the water's surface and snatches fish using its sharp, curved claws. It can catch up to 30 fish in one night.

SIZE 2–3 in (6–8 cm) long

DIET Fish, crabs, and insects

HABITAT Forests, rivers, streams, and wetlands

DISTRIBUTION Central America and South America

Common vampire bat

Desmodus rotundus

The common vampire bat feeds on blood. It bites its prey with razor-sharp incisor teeth and drinks the blood that flows from the wound. A special substance in its saliva prevents the blood from clotting while the bat is feeding.

SIZE 2¾–3¾ in (7–9.5 cm) long

DIET Blood of birds, tapirs, and farm animals

HABITAT Tropical forests, deserts, grasslands, and human settlements

DISTRIBUTION Central America and South America

Long forelimb

California leaf-nosed bat

Macrotus californicus

This bat usually flies a few meters above the ground and comes closer to the surface to capture prey. It hovers above its prey for a few seconds before snatching it off the ground or off foliage.

SIZE 2–2½ in (5–6.5 cm) long

DIET Insects

HABITAT Deserts and scrublands

DISTRIBUTION North America and Central America

Common pipistrelle

Pipistrellus pipistrellus

In the summer, female pipistrelles form large roosts to give birth to young and look after them. Males roost on their own or in small groups through this period.

SIZE 1½–1¾ in (3.5–4.5 cm) long

DIET Insects

HABITAT Temperate forests

DISTRIBUTION Europe to northern Africa and western and central Asia

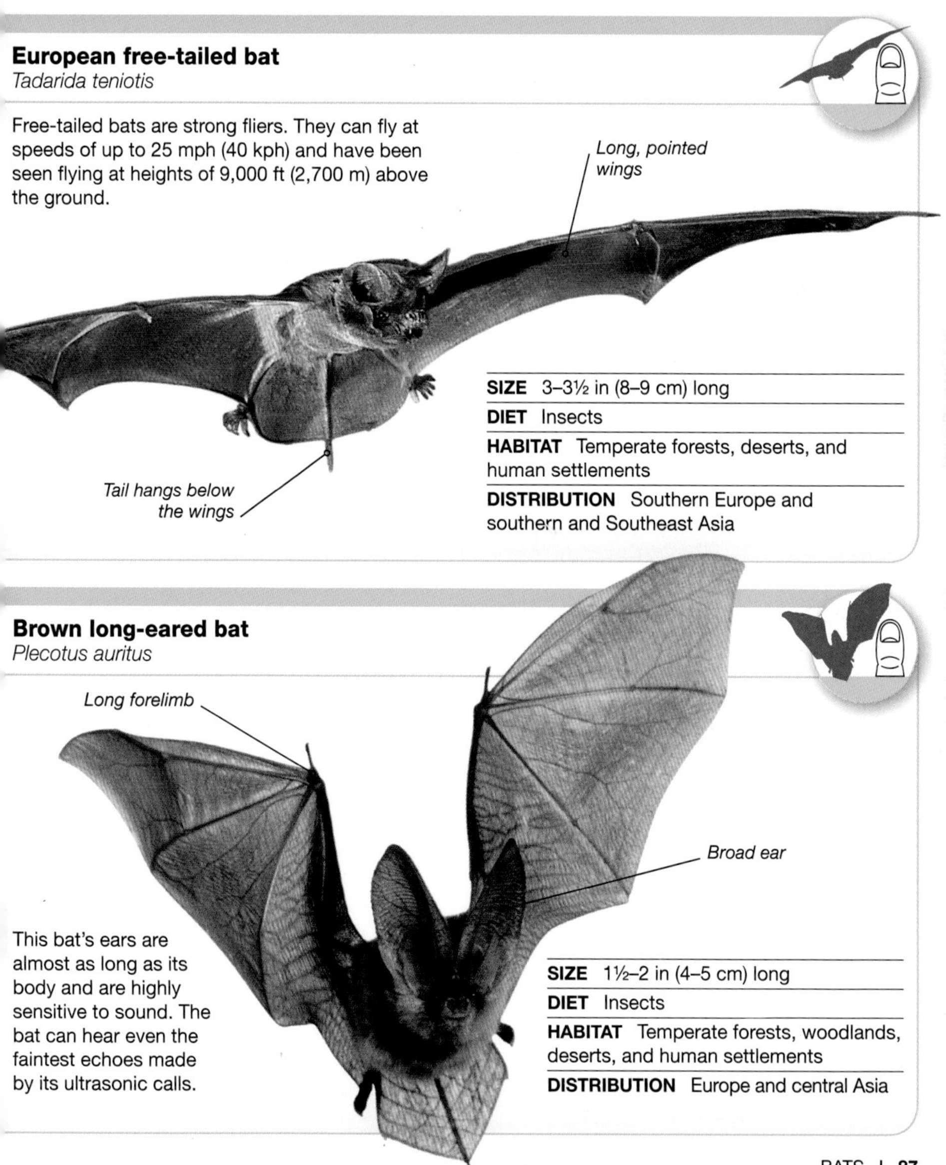

European free-tailed bat

Tadarida teniotis

Free-tailed bats are strong fliers. They can fly at speeds of up to 25 mph (40 kph) and have been seen flying at heights of 9,000 ft (2,700 m) above the ground.

SIZE 3–3½ in (8–9 cm) long

DIET Insects

HABITAT Temperate forests, deserts, and human settlements

DISTRIBUTION Southern Europe and southern and Southeast Asia

Brown long-eared bat

Plecotus auritus

This bat's ears are almost as long as its body and are highly sensitive to sound. The bat can hear even the faintest echoes made by its ultrasonic calls.

SIZE 1½–2 in (4–5 cm) long

DIET Insects

HABITAT Temperate forests, woodlands, deserts, and human settlements

DISTRIBUTION Europe and central Asia

In flight, a bat's heart beats

1,000 times

every minute

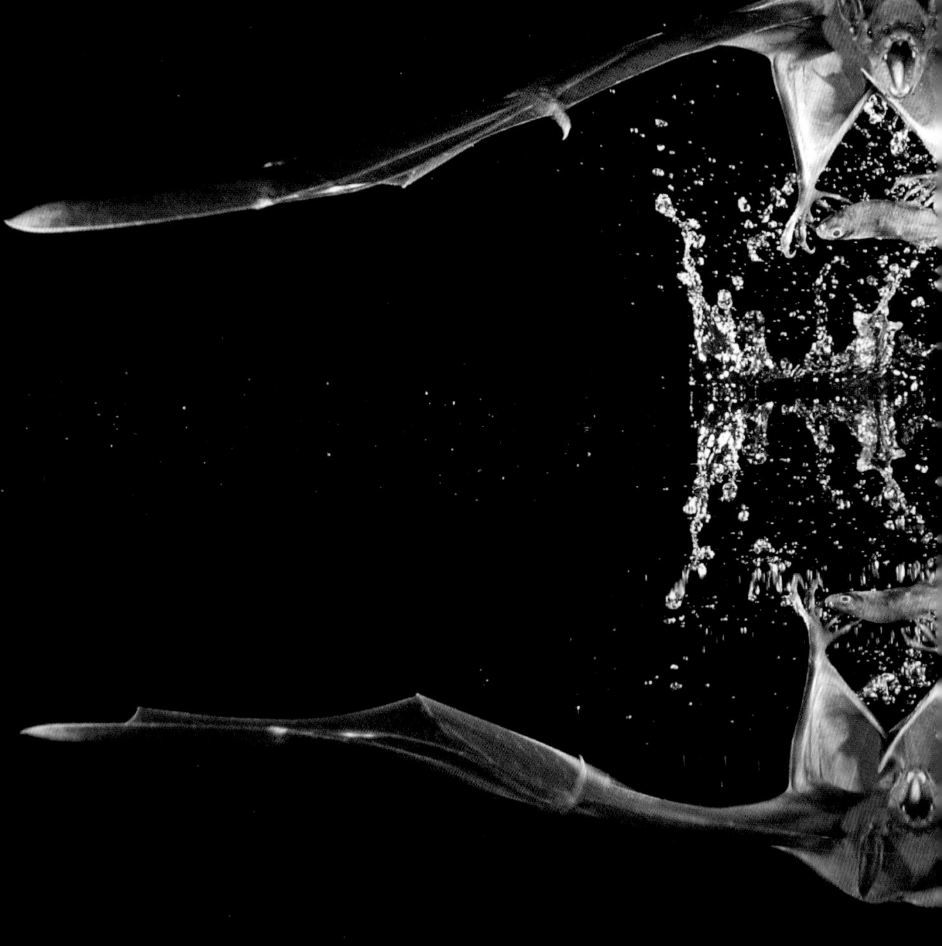

GREATER BULLDOG BAT

Also known as the fishing bat, the greater bulldog bat preys mainly on fish. Once it has snatched a fish, it quickly pulls its victim to its mouth to prevent it from escaping. The bat then hangs itself upside down from a tree and eats its prey headfirst.

Moonrats, hedgehogs, and pangolins

The 24 species of hedgehog and moonrat, which form the order Erinaceomorpha, are mostly active at night. Pangolins are also mainly nocturnal and are covered in scales. The eight known species form the order Pholidota.

Moonrat

Echinosorex gymnura

The moonrat smells like rotting onions. It uses this scent to mark its territory, warning other moonrats to stay away.

SIZE 10–18 in (26–46 cm) long

DIET Snails, earthworms, crabs, fish, and fruit

HABITAT Tropical forests

DISTRIBUTION Southeast Asia

European hedgehog

Erinaceus europaeus

An adult hedgehog's body is covered in more than 5,000 sharp spines. When threatened, it raises its spines and curls into a tight, prickly ball. It sometimes licks its spines, smearing them with its foamy saliva, although the reason for this is still a mystery.

SIZE 8½–10½ in (22–27 cm) long

DIET Small reptiles, birds' eggs, and carrion

HABITAT Temperate forests, woodlands, grasslands, and human settlements

DISTRIBUTION Europe

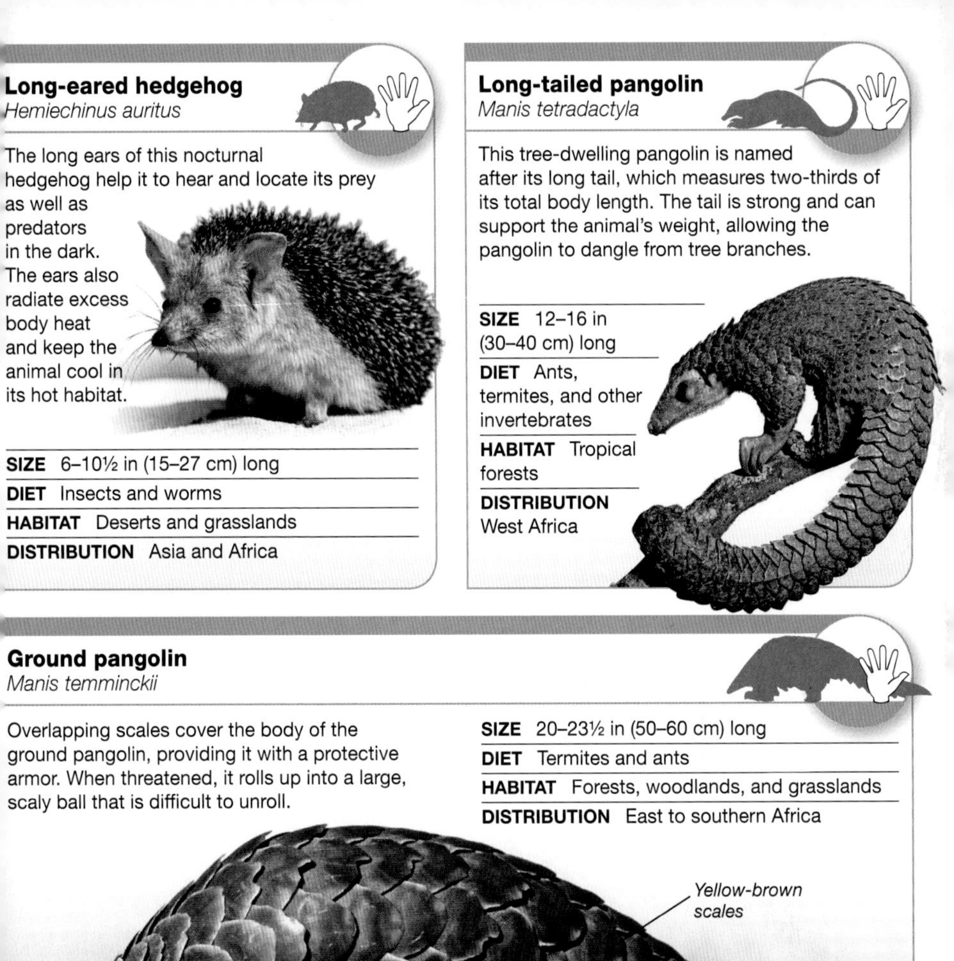

Long-eared hedgehog
Hemiechinus auritus

The long ears of this nocturnal hedgehog help it to hear and locate its prey as well as predators in the dark. The ears also radiate excess body heat and keep the animal cool in its hot habitat.

SIZE 6–10½ in (15–27 cm) long
DIET Insects and worms
HABITAT Deserts and grasslands
DISTRIBUTION Asia and Africa

Long-tailed pangolin
Manis tetradactyla

This tree-dwelling pangolin is named after its long tail, which measures two-thirds of its total body length. The tail is strong and can support the animal's weight, allowing the pangolin to dangle from tree branches.

SIZE 12–16 in (30–40 cm) long
DIET Ants, termites, and other invertebrates
HABITAT Tropical forests
DISTRIBUTION West Africa

Ground pangolin
Manis temminckii

Overlapping scales cover the body of the ground pangolin, providing it with a protective armor. When threatened, it rolls up into a large, scaly ball that is difficult to unroll.

SIZE 20–23½ in (50–60 cm) long
DIET Termites and ants
HABITAT Forests, woodlands, and grasslands
DISTRIBUTION East to southern Africa

Yellow-brown scales

Shrews, moles, and solenodons

A long snout, sharp teeth, and small eyes are common to more than 400 species of mole, shrew, and solenodon that make up the order Soricomorpha.

Eurasian water shrew

Neomys fodiens

This tiny shrew can stay underwater for up to 20 seconds at a time while searching for its food. It swims by kicking hard with its hind feet and steers itself using its long tail.

SIZE 2½–3¾ in (6.5–9.5 cm) long

DIET Insects, small fish, and frogs

HABITAT Forests, wetlands, rivers, and streams

DISTRIBUTION Europe to northern Asia

Hispaniolan solenodon

Solenodon paradoxus

ENDANGERED

This shrewlike solenodon is one of the few venomous mammals. The venom is released with its saliva, giving this animal a venomous bite, which it mainly uses to defend itself.

SIZE 11–12½ in (28–32 cm) long

DIET Insects, worms, small reptiles, and fruit

HABITAT Tropical forests

DISTRIBUTION Hispaniola island, Caribbean

Long tail

European mole

Talpa europaea

The European mole is almost blind and finds its prey using its senses of touch, smell, and hearing. It moves toward prey by scooping up soil to the sides with its front legs, while anchoring itself with its hind legs.

SIZE 4½–6½ in (11–16 cm) long

DIET Insects and worms

HABITAT Temperate forests and grasslands

DISTRIBUTION Europe to northern Asia

Pyrenean desman

Galemys pyrenaicus

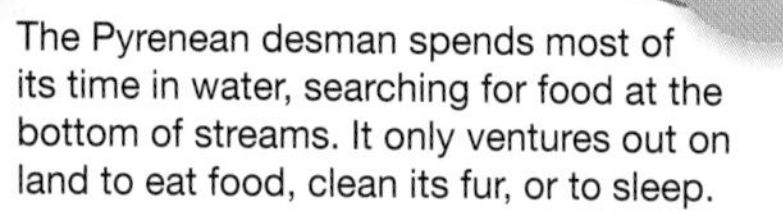

The Pyrenean desman spends most of its time in water, searching for food at the bottom of streams. It only ventures out on land to eat food, clean its fur, or to sleep.

SIZE 4½–6½ in (11–16 cm) long

DIET Small crustaceans and insect larvae

HABITAT Wetlands, rivers, and streams

DISTRIBUTION Southwestern Europe

Star-nosed mole

Condylura cristata

This mole is named after the circle of 22 fleshy tentacles around its nose that looks like a star. These tentacles are covered in special sensory receptors called Eimer's organs and help it identify prey by touch.

SIZE 7–7½ in (18–19 cm) long

DIET Insects, earthworms, and small fish

HABITAT Wetlands, rivers, and streams

DISTRIBUTION North America

Carnivores

These mammals belong to the order Carnivora, which contains about 285 species. Most of these species are meat-eating predators, such as seals, dogs, and cats.

FOCUS ON...
PATTERNS

Different species of carnivore can be recognized by the unique patterns on their fur.

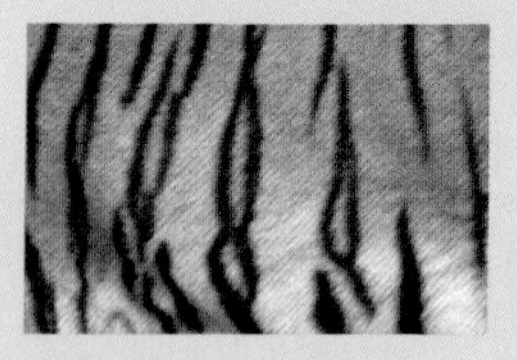

▲ The tiger's fur has distinctive stripes.

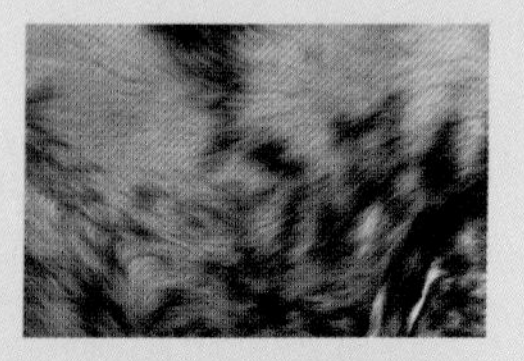

▲ The African wild dog's fur coat has patches in black, gray, yellow, and white.

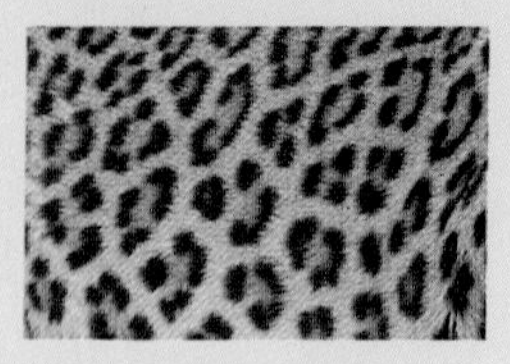

▲ The leopard can be identified easily by the spots covering its body.

African wild dog
Lycaon pictus

ENDANGERED

African wild dogs live in groups of 30 or more individuals that are called packs. Only the dominant pair breeds, while the other members of the pack help look after the pups.

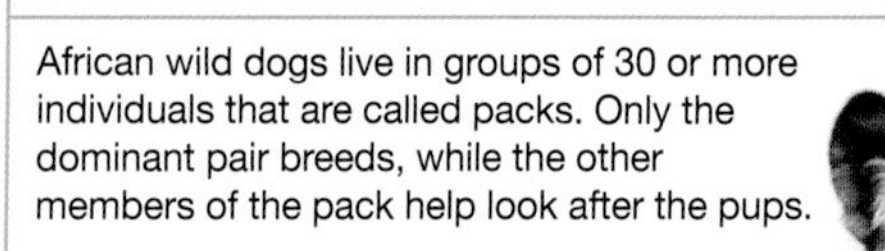

SIZE 30–43 in (76–110 cm) long

DIET Rodents, birds, and other mammals

HABITAT Mountains, grasslands, and coastal areas

DISTRIBUTION Africa

Red fox

Vulpes vulpes

The adaptable red fox is equally at home in urban areas and in the wild. It is often seen scavenging from trash cans in urban areas to supplement its usual diet of small mammals, such as rodents.

SIZE 23–36 in (58–90 cm) long

DIET Mainly small mammals

HABITAT Mainly human settlements

DISTRIBUTION Northern hemisphere and Australia

Maned wolf

Chrysocyon brachyurus

Long legs give the maned wolf a good height. This allows the wolf to peer above the tall grasses of South America's grasslands when hunting for prey.

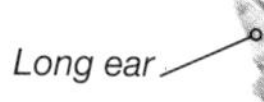

SIZE 4–4¼ ft (1.2–1.3 m) long

DIET Birds, fish, rodents, rabbits, invertebrates, and fruit

HABITAT Grasslands

DISTRIBUTION South America

Fennec fox

Vulpes zerda

This tiny fox is well adapted to life in the desert. Its pale coat camouflages the animal in the sand. The coat also reflects the Sun's heat, while its large ears radiate excess body heat.

SIZE 10–16 in (24–41 cm) long

DIET Fruit, seeds, eggs, termites, and lizards

HABITAT Deserts

DISTRIBUTION Northern Africa

Raccoon dog

Nyctereutes procyonoides

The raccoon dog eats large amounts of food in the fall and increases its body weight by up to 50 percent, after which it hibernates through the cold winter months, usually in an old den of a fox or a badger.

SIZE 20–23½ in (50–60 cm) long

DIET Fruit, birds, rodents, and fish

HABITAT Forests, rivers, streams, and wetlands

DISTRIBUTION Europe and Asia

Gray wolf

Canis lupus

Gray wolves live in large groups, called packs. Members of a pack use various signals to communicate with each other. A raised tail and stiff legs show dominance, for example, while snarls indicate aggression.

SIZE 3¼–5 ft (1–1.5 m) long

DIET Mainly deer, rabbits, and rodents

HABITAT Temperate forests, mountains, and tundra

DISTRIBUTION
North America, Greenland, Europe, and Asia

The gray wolf is the ancestor of all breeds of domestic dog in the world.

Black-backed jackal

Canis mesomelas

This mammal has a keen sense of hearing. It often listens to the sounds made by invertebrates, such as insects burrowing underground, and quickly digs them out to eat.

SIZE 16–36 in (45–90 cm) long

DIET Small reptiles, birds, invertebrates, and carrion

HABITAT Deserts, grasslands, and human settlements

DISTRIBUTION
East and southern Africa

Domestic dog

Canis lupus familiaris

Different breeds of domestic dog, such as this bloodhound, are all members of the same subspecies. The bloodhound is known for its keen sense of smell, which is about 10,000 times more sensitive than that of a human.

SIZE 23–27 in (58–69 cm) long

DIET Mainly meat

HABITAT Human settlements

DISTRIBUTION
Worldwide except polar regions

Dingo

Canis lupus dingo

The dingo is a wild dog that roams freely in Australia and is now the continent's top predator. It is often considered a pest because it preys on farm animals, especially sheep. Australian shepherds build long fences to keep out dingoes, and some of these can run for thousands of miles.

SIZE 28¼–43 in (72–110 cm) long

DIET Wallabies, small kangaroos, rabbits, rodents, and livestock

HABITAT Forests and grasslands

DISTRIBUTION Australia

Pale underside

Coyote

Canis latrans

Although coyotes live in packs of up to seven members, they usually hunt alone, or in pairs. They make a number of distinctive howls and high-pitched barks to call pack members back together after hunting and to warn off rival packs.

SIZE 27½–38 in (70–97 cm) long

DIET Rodents, rabbits, lizards, fruit, and livestock

HABITAT Forests, mountains, grasslands, tundra, and human settlements

DISTRIBUTION North America and Central America

Asiatic black bear

Ursus thibetanus

This bear is a good climber. It spends more than half of its life in trees, foraging for food and seeking shelter. On the ground, it can stand upright and walk on two legs for about half a mile—a habit that is unusual for bears.

SIZE 4¼–6¼ ft (1.3–1.9 m) long

DIET Nuts, fruit, leaves, grass, herbs, insects, and grubs

HABITAT Forests and mountains

DISTRIBUTION Eastern, southern, and Southeast Asia

"V" shaped white patch on chest

Sharp claws help in climbing trees

Fur is mostly dark brown, but the color may vary between individuals

Polar bear

Ursus maritimus

The polar bear is the largest predator on land and mostly hunts seals. It stalks seals resting on the ice, using the camouflage provided by its white fur. It may also wait for seals to surface at their breathing holes in the ice, before grabbing one and killing it with its powerful bite.

SIZE 7–11 ft (2.1–3.4 m) long

DIET Mainly seals

HABITAT Polar regions, coastal areas, and seas

DISTRIBUTION Arctic Ocean and northern Canada

Brown bear

Ursus arctos

Some brown bears prey on salmon when they swim to freshwater to spawn (lay eggs). Once caught, the bears kill the fish with a powerful bite or a blow from their paws. A bear will often eat only the most nutritious parts of a salmon, such as its brain.

SIZE 6½–10 ft (2–3 m) long

DIET Leaves, fruit, berries, roots, tubers, insects, small mammals, and fish

HABITAT Forests, woodlands, grasslands, mountains, and semideserts

DISTRIBUTION Northern Asia

Long claws dig out food and grip slippery fish

A polar bear's fur is not white. Each hair is a translucent tube, which reflects light in a way that makes the bear look white.

Large paws spread the weight of the bear, preventing it from slipping on the ice

Arctic foxes are the only members of the dog family that

change color

between summer and winter

ARCTIC FOX

The pure white coat of the Arctic fox makes it almost invisible against the snow in winter. This camouflages the animal against predators and also hides it from prey, allowing it to hunt with ease. In the spring, when the snow melts, the animal's coat turns gray or blue.

California sea lion

Zalophus californianus

Small ear

California sea lions are intelligent mammals that are well-known for their ability to learn new things. They have long been major attractions in amusement parks, where they have been taught to perform a number of tricks, such as balancing balls on their noses.

SIZE Up to 8 ft (2.4 m) long

DIET Mainly fish

HABITAT Coastal areas

DISTRIBUTION Western US

Baikal seal

Phoca sibirica

This species of freshwater seal is also known as the nerpa. It is found only in Lake Baikal in Russia. Some scientists think that its ancestors probably swam upriver to the area from Arctic waters thousands of years ago.

SIZE 4–4½ ft (1.2–1.4 m) long

DIET Sculpins (spiny fish)

HABITAT Lakes

DISTRIBUTION Eastern Asia

Walrus

Odobenus rosmarus

The walrus can dive to depths greater than 330 ft (100 m) to search for food. It roots through sediment with its snout, using its whiskers to find prey. The walrus may also squirt water from its mouth or wave its foreflippers to uncover prey hidden in the seabed.

SIZE 10–12 ft (3–3.6 m) long

DIET Worms, shellfish, sea snails, shrimp, and fish

HABITAT Shallow seas, coastal areas, and polar regions

DISTRIBUTION Arctic Ocean

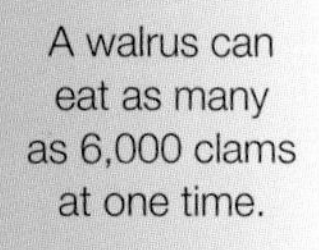

Rough, wrinkly skin

Long tusk is used by males to fight rivals during the breeding season

Northern raccoon

Procyon lotor

Raccoons are not fussy in their choice of food and will eat almost anything. They use their front paws, which are highly sensitive to touch, to examine their food before eating it.

SIZE 16–25½ in (40–65 cm) long

DIET Fruit, small mammals, and insects

HABITAT Mainly woodlands and scrublands

DISTRIBUTION North America to Central America

Striped skunk

Mephitis mephitis

When threatened, the striped skunk fluffs its fur, arches its back, and lifts it tail. If this does not deter the predator, it stands on its front feet, twists its body, and ejects a foul-smelling liquid from glands under its tail.

SIZE 21½–29½ in (55–75 cm) long

DIET Insects, birds, fish, mollusks, and fruit

HABITAT Forests and human settlements

DISTRIBUTION North America and Central America

Red panda

Ailurus fulgens

Like the giant panda, the red panda's diet consists mostly of a plant called bamboo. However, unlike the giant panda, which eats every part of a bamboo plant except the roots, the red panda only eats the most tender shoots and leaves. It can spend up to 13 hours in a day searching for and feeding on bamboo.

SIZE 20–25 in (50–64 cm) long

DIET Mainly bamboo, but also fruit, grubs, small reptiles, birds' eggs and chicks, and small mammals

HABITAT Forests and mountains

DISTRIBUTION Southern to Southeast Asia

Least weasel

Mustela nivalis

The least weasel is the smallest member of the order Carnivora and usually feeds on small mammals, such as rodents. It has a long, thin body, which allows it to slip easily into the burrows of rodents to prey on them. The animal eats about half its body weight in meat every day.

SIZE 4½–10 in (11–26 cm) long

DIET Mainly mice

HABITAT Forests, mountains, grasslands, and polar regions

DISTRIBUTION North America, Greenland, Europe, and northern, central, and eastern Asia

Fur turns white in the winter, and camouflages against snow

European pine marten
Martes martes

The European pine marten climbs deftly through trees, using its bushy tail to balance itself on branches. Although an agile climber, it mostly hunts on the ground.

SIZE 16–21½ in (40–55 cm) long

DIET Rodents, birds, insects, and fruit

HABITAT Temperate and coniferous forests

DISTRIBUTION Europe; western and northern Asia

Giant otter
Pteronura brasiliensis

Eurasian badger
Meles meles

Eurasian badgers live in groups called clans. Each clan has six or more members—one dominant male, one or more females, and the cubs. Clans live together in a large system of underground tunnels called setts.

SIZE 22–35 in (56–90 cm) long

DIET Mainly earthworms

HABITAT Temperate forests

DISTRIBUTION Europe to western Asia

Sea otter
Enhydra lutris

The sea otter lives in cold waters and has a dense coat of fur covering its body. The coat of an adult sea otter can have more than 800 million hairs. These hairs trap warm air close to its body and help it to stay warm.

SIZE 21½–51 in (55–130 cm) long

DIET Crabs, clams, and sea urchins

HABITAT Coastal areas, seas, and oceans

DISTRIBUTION North Pacific

ENDANGERED

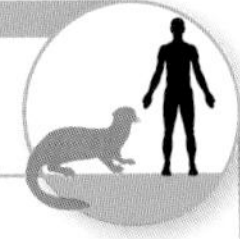

Giant otters are among the top predators in South America. They prey on aquatic animals and mainly on fish. These mammals use their sharp eyesight to spot their prey. They then chase after it and seize it with their powerful forepaws before eating it from the head down.

SIZE 3¼–4½ ft (1–1.4 m) long

DIET Fish, crabs, shrimp, and aquatic insects

HABITAT Rain forests, wetlands, rivers, and streams

DISTRIBUTION South America

Wolverine

Gulo gulo

This predator lives in cold regions and feeds on frozen carcasses in the winter. Its powerful jaws and large teeth help it to crush the frozen meat and bones it eats.

SIZE 25½–41 in (65–105 cm) long

DIET Deer, hare, mice, birds, birds' eggs, carrion, and fruit

HABITAT Forests, mountains, and polar regions

DISTRIBUTION Canada, northwestern North America, northern Europe, and northern and eastern Asia

The wolverine can travel 30 miles (50 km) in a day in search of food.

Fossa
Cryptoprocta ferox

The top predator in Madagascar (an island off the southeastern coast of Africa), the fossa is an excellent climber and uses its tail to balance itself when moving through trees. It hunts by day as well as at night. It used to prey mainly on lemurs, but now also attacks livestock when available.

SIZE 23½–30 in (60–76 cm) long

DIET Mainly lemurs

HABITAT Tropical forests

DISTRIBUTION Madagascar

Banded mongoose
Mungos mungo

Small spotted genet
Genetta genetta

This nocturnal species has a gray coat with black spots and a black-and-gray striped tail. Females give birth to two litters a year, each containing up to four cubs. The cubs start communicating with their mother using a call that sounds like a hiccup.

Long, striped tail

Banded mongooses live in groups of up to 20 individuals. They breed about four times a year and the females in the group tend to give birth on or around the same day. Males often babysit the pups while other members go foraging.

SIZE 12–18 in (30–45 cm) long

DIET Insects, birds, birds' eggs and chicks, snails, and fruit

HABITAT Savanna

DISTRIBUTION Sub-Saharan Africa

SIZE 16–21½ in (40–55 cm) long

DIET Small mammals, birds, grubs, and fruit

HABITAT Forests, savanna, and farmlands

DISTRIBUTION Africa and southwestern Europe

Meerkat

Suricata suricatta

Meerkats live in groups of 20–40 individuals. One or more members of the group stand guard on mounds or bushes to watch out for danger. These are the sentries and they follow the group of meerkats that forage. While the other members eat, the sentries stay alert and bark an alarm on spotting an attacker.

SIZE 10–14 in (25–35 cm) long

DIET Mainly insects, spiders, and small reptiles

HABITAT Deserts and semideserts

DISTRIBUTION Southern Africa

Standing on two hind legs helps the animal to see farther

Domestic cat

Felis catus

All kinds of domestic cat, such as the Siamese cat, are members of the same species. Humans bred the first domestic cats in the Middle East as far back as 10,000 years ago.

SIZE 14–20 in (35–50 cm) long

DIET Mainly meat

HABITAT Human settlements

DISTRIBUTION Worldwide except polar regions

Serval

Leptailurus serval

This large-eared cat has a sharp sense of hearing and finds its prey by listening for the sound of moving animals. Once it has found its target, the serval jumps up and pounces on its prey with powerful forepaws. It is also known to leap up and take birds from the air.

SIZE 23½–39 in (60–100 cm) long

DIET Rodents, birds, fish, frogs, and large insects

HABITAT Grasslands and wetlands

DISTRIBUTION Sub-Saharan Africa

Margay

Leopardus wiedii

The margay spends most of its time on trees. It is the only member of the cat family that can rotate its hind feet almost completely outward, allowing it to climb down trees headfirst.

SIZE 18–31 in (46–79 cm) long

DIET Small mammals, small birds, grubs, and spiders

HABITAT Tropical forests

DISTRIBUTION Southern North America, Central America, and South America

Markings on fur help to camouflage the animal in shady trees

Long neck gives it the nickname "giraffe cat"

Bobcat

Lynx rufus

Bobcats live on their own. The home territory of each bobcat stretches over several miles and never overlaps with the territory of another bobcat of the same gender.

SIZE 26–43 in (65–110 cm) long

DIET Mainly rabbits, other mammals, and birds

HABITAT Forests, deserts, and woodlands

DISTRIBUTION North America and Mexico

Caracal

Caracal caracal

The caracal is well-known for its speed and agility. It can leap up to 10 ft (3 m) in the air to snatch a bird flying by. It is also the fastest cat of its size and can run down prey such as small antelopes and hares.

SIZE 23½–36 in (60–91 cm) long

DIET Small mammals and farm animals

HABITAT Scrublands, deserts, and mountains

DISTRIBUTION Africa and southern Asia

Lion

Panthera leo

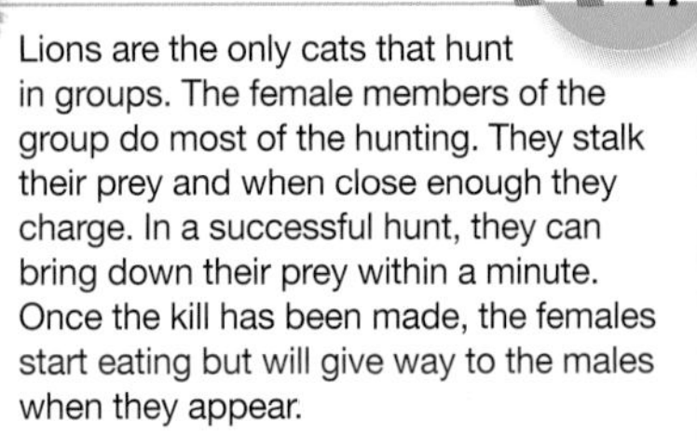

Lions are the only cats that hunt in groups. The female members of the group do most of the hunting. They stalk their prey and when close enough they charge. In a successful hunt, they can bring down their prey within a minute. Once the kill has been made, the females start eating but will give way to the males when they appear.

SIZE 5½–8¼ ft (1.7–2.5 m) long

DIET Large mammals, such as zebras, impala, and wildebeest

HABITAT Forests, savanna, and deserts

DISTRIBUTION Africa and northwestern India

Tiger

Panthera tigris

ENDANGERED

The tiger is the largest of the big cats. An adult male may weigh up to 660 lb (300 kg), but can chase after prey with surprising agility. It can also leap up to 33 ft (10 m) in one jump.

SIZE 4½–9 ft (1.4–2.8 m) long

DIET Mainly deer and wild pigs

HABITAT Forests and mountains

DISTRIBUTION Southern and eastern Asia

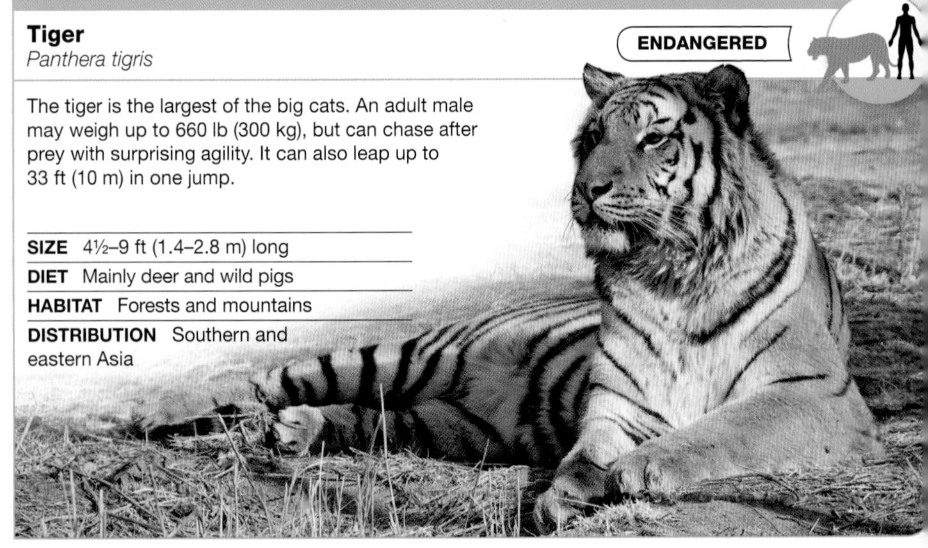

Jaguar

Panthera onca

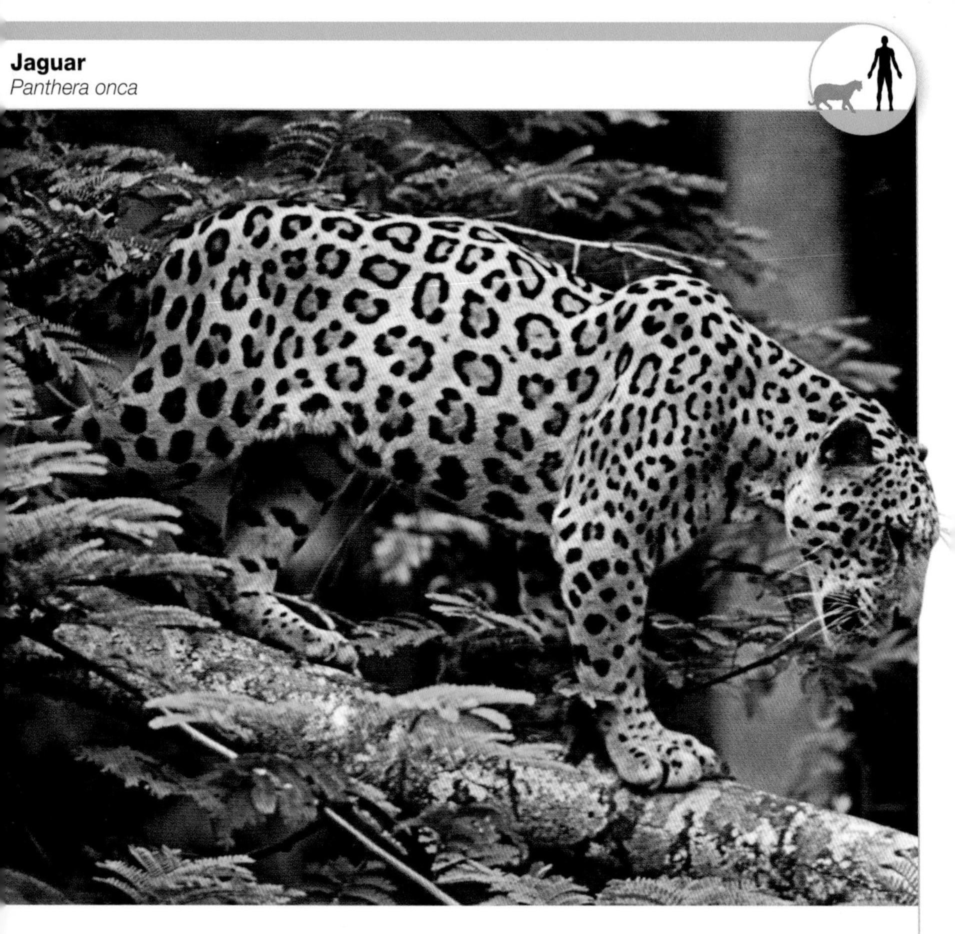

This big cat has a powerful bite and an unusual way of killing its prey. Instead of suffocating its prey by strangling it, the jaguar sometimes bites through the skull of its victim. When hunting river turtles, it bites through the shells of the turtles with its large canine teeth.

SIZE 3½–6¼ ft (1.1–1.9 m) long

DIET Deer, tapirs, and peccaries

HABITAT Rain forests, wetlands, and grasslands

DISTRIBUTION Central America and South America

Puma
Puma concolor

The puma's long and powerful hind legs make it an agile leaper. It can jump as high as 15 ft (5 m) and as far as 20 ft (6 m).

SIZE 3½–6½ ft (1.1–2 m) long

DIET Small mammals

HABITAT Forests, mountains, deserts, and grasslands

DISTRIBUTION North America, Central America, and South America

Snow leopard
Uncia uncia

ENDANGERED

This big cat uses its long tail to keep its balance. When it sleeps, the tail covers its paws and face, protecting it from the freezing winds in its habitat.

SIZE 3–4¼ ft (1–1.3 m) long

DIET Wild sheep, goats, marmots, pikas, hares, and birds

HABITAT Mountains

DISTRIBUTION Asia

Cheetah

Acinonyx jubatus

Cheetahs leave home between the ages of 13 and 20 months. Brothers may continue living together, forming small, permanent groups known as coalitions. The females tend to live on their own and come together with the males only to mate.

SIZE 3½–5 ft (1.1–1.5 m) long

DIET Hoofed mammals, such as gazelles and antelopes

HABITAT Deserts and grasslands

DISTRIBUTION Africa and western Asia

It takes the cheetah—the world's fastest land mammal—only 60 seconds to close in on its prey.

The snow leopard

cannot roar,

but communicates through

hisses and growls

SNOW LEOPARD

The snow leopard is well adapted to living on cold, rocky mountains. Its grayish, long-haired coat keeps this predator warm and camouflages it among the gray rocks around it. Wide paws with furry undersides allow it to walk easily on the cold, slippery slopes.

Aardwolf

Proteles cristata

Unlike other hyenas that prey on large animals, the aardwolf licks termites from the ground with its long, sticky tongue. It can eat up to 300,000 termites in a day.

SIZE 26 in (67 cm) long

DIET Mainly termites

HABITAT Scrublands and deserts

DISTRIBUTION East and southern Africa

Striped hyena

Hyaena hyaena

Scavengers are animals that feed on dead and decaying animal matter, or carrion. The striped hyena is a master scavenger—it mainly feeds on carcasses and little is left once it has eaten. Its powerful digestive system can break down skin, bones, teeth, and even hooves.

SIZE 3½ ft (1.1 m) long

DIET Mainly carrion; also fruit and vegetables

HABITAT Grasslands, mountains, and deserts

DISTRIBUTION East, west, and northern Africa, and western to southern Asia

Forefeet are larger than hind feet

Spotted hyena

Crocuta crocuta

The spotted hyena can make up to 14 different calls to express different emotions. It is also called the "laughing hyena" because one of its best-known calls sounds similar to human laughter.

SIZE 4¼ ft (1.3 m) long

DIET Other mammals, fish, birds, and carrion

HABITAT Savanna, mountains, and deserts

DISTRIBUTION Sub-Saharan Africa

Brown hyena

Parahyaena brunnea

The brown hyena lives in groups but forages alone. It produces pastelike secretions from a gland below its tail. These secretions are used to mark out an individual's foraging territory and inform group members about an individual hyena's location.

SIZE 4¼ ft (1.3 m) long

DIET Mainly carrion, but also fruit

HABITAT Savanna, deserts, and mountains

DISTRIBUTION Southern Africa

Odd-toed ungulates

Ungulates are hoofed mammals. The order Perissodactyla includes large, hoofed grazers, such as rhinoceroses, tapirs, and horses, with an odd number of toes.

FOCUS ON... **DEFENSE**

Odd-toed ungulates use different body parts to defend themselves against predators.

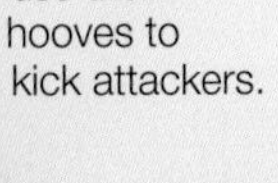

◀ Horses use their hooves to kick attackers.

▲ The white-horned rhinoceros uses its horns to defend itself.

▲ A zebra's stripes act as camouflage—a pattern that makes it harder for predators to see it.

Kiang

Equus kiang

The kiang is one of the largest of the Asian equids (members of the horse family) that live on plateaus. Its habitat remains cold for most of the year. In the winter it grows a reddish-brown woolly coat that protects it from the cold.

Dark stripe on the back

SIZE 4½–5 ft (1.4–1.5 m) long

DIET Grass and sedges

HABITAT Grasslands, deserts, and hills

DISTRIBUTION Tibetan plateau in Asia

Grevy's zebra

Equus grevyi

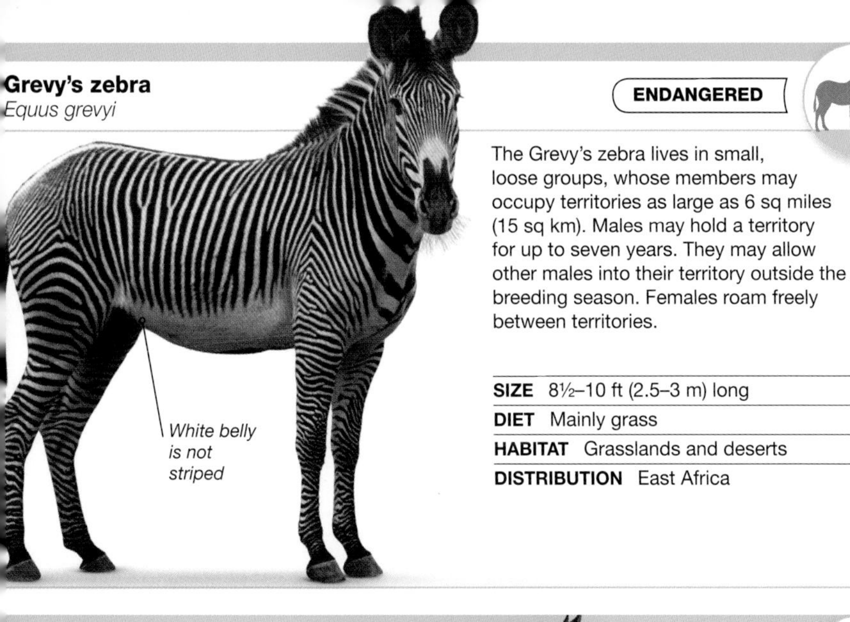

ENDANGERED

The Grevy's zebra lives in small, loose groups, whose members may occupy territories as large as 6 sq miles (15 sq km). Males may hold a territory for up to seven years. They may allow other males into their territory outside the breeding season. Females roam freely between territories.

SIZE 8½–10 ft (2.5–3 m) long

DIET Mainly grass

HABITAT Grasslands and deserts

DISTRIBUTION East Africa

Domestic horse

Equus ferus caballus

Humans domesticated the wild horse about 9,000 years ago and created many different breeds, such as the Arab horse. Horses have been used for warfare, plowing, hauling heavy loads, riding over long distances, rounding up cattle, and in racing.

Hoof has single toe

SIZE 5–5¼ ft (1.5–1.6 m) long

DIET Grass, leaves, and buds

HABITAT Human settlements

DISTRIBUTION Worldwide except tropical forests and polar regions

Indian rhinoceros

Rhinoceros unicornis

Tough layers of skin cover the entire body of an adult Indian rhinoceros, including its tail. This protective, armorlike skin makes it almost impossible for an adult rhinoceros to be targeted by predators in the wild. However, sick and old rhinoceroses are known to be killed by tigers.

SIZE Up to 12½ ft (3.8 m) long

DIET Mainly tall grass

HABITAT Grasslands

DISTRIBUTION Southern Asia

White rhinoceros

Ceratotherium simum

The largest of all rhinoceroses, this species is also the largest mammal on land after the elephants. In spite of weighing up to 2.5 tons (2.3 metric tons), it can run remarkably fast—at speeds of up to 25 mph (40 kph)—and can make quick changes in direction while running.

SIZE 12–13 ft (3.7–4 m) long

DIET Mainly grass

HABITAT Savanna

DISTRIBUTION East and southern Africa

Malayan tapir
Tapirus indicus

ENDANGERED

Like all species of tapir, the Malayan tapir has a grasping, trunklike snout. It curls its snout around clumps of twigs and leaves and draws them into its mouth.

SIZE 6–8¼ ft (1.8–2.5 m) long

DIET Twigs, leaves, and fallen fruit

HABITAT
Rain forests

DISTRIBUTION
Southeast Asia

Three toes on hind foot

Four toes on forefoot

Even-toed ungulates

The order Artiodactyla is made up of a diverse group of hoofed mammals that have an even number of toes on each foot. This group has more than 350 species and includes pigs, camels, deer, giraffes, antelopes, sheep, goats, cattle, and hippopotamuses.

Wild boar
Sus scrofa

This mammal forages for food from dawn to dusk in a wide range of habitats. It has a good long-term memory and remembers areas rich in food.

SIZE 3–6 ft (0.9–1.8 m) long
DIET Fruit, seeds, roots, insects, and lizards
HABITAT Forests and wetlands
DISTRIBUTION Europe, Asia, and northern Africa

Hippopotamus
Hippopotamus amphibius

The word *hippopotamus* comes from the Greek for "river horse." Like horses on land, this animal can move gracefully in water. Its body is heavier than water, so it sinks and walks along the bottom of rivers and lakes. Its eyes and nostrils are located on top of its head, allowing it to see and breathe even when the rest of its body is submerged in water.

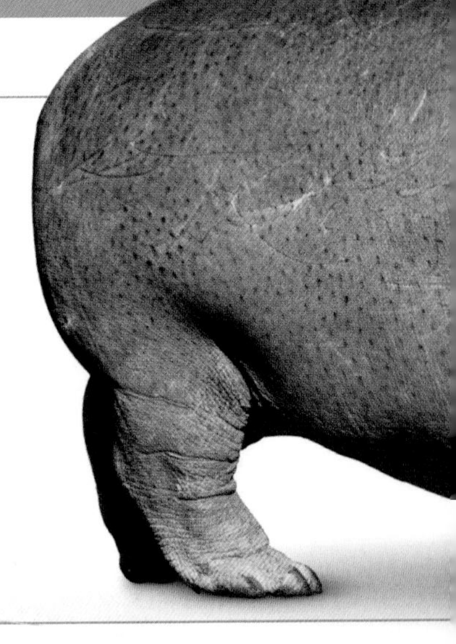

SIZE 9 ft (2.7 m) long
DIET Mainly grass
HABITAT Grasslands, wetlands, rivers, and streams
DISTRIBUTION Africa

Warthog

Phacochoerus africanus

When resting, the warthog allows the banded mongoose to eat insects from its skin. In doing so the mongoose also removes any external parasites from the skin. This helps the warthog get rid of bothersome ticks while the mongoose gets a good meal.

SIZE 3–5 ft (0.9–1.5 m) long

DIET Grass and underground stems

HABITAT Open woodlands, savanna, and scrublands

DISTRIBUTION Sub-Saharan Africa

Four toes

Skin produces a reddish fluid that acts as a natural sunscreen by keeping the animal's skin moist

Four webbed toes

Guanaco
Lama guanicoe

Guanacos live in herds made up of a dominant male, females, and infants. When a member of a herd senses danger, it makes a high-pitched warning call, signaling the others to flee. The dominant male usually runs behind the group to protect its members.

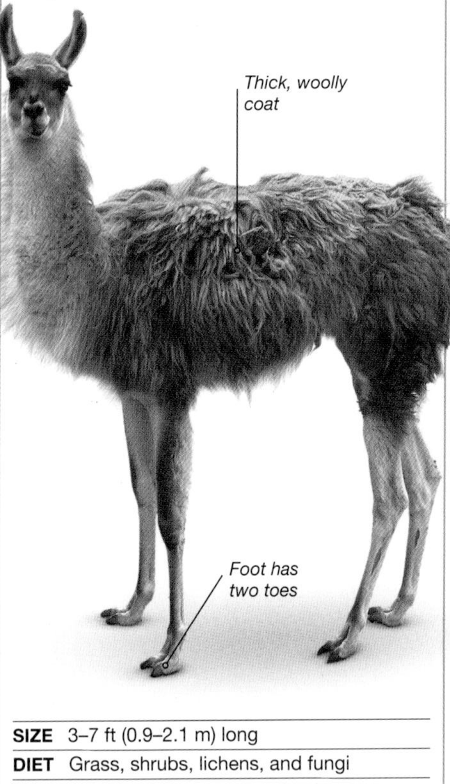

SIZE 3–7 ft (0.9–2.1 m) long

DIET Grass, shrubs, lichens, and fungi

HABITAT Mountains, grasslands, deserts, and forests

DISTRIBUTION South America

Bactrian camel
Camelus bactrianus

ENDANGERED

This mammal can live with little or no food and water for long periods of time. The two humps on its back store fat from the food it eats. When food is not available, the stored fat is converted to energy to keep the animal's body going. This helps the Bactrian camel to stay alive in harsh deserts.

SIZE 8¼–10 ft (2.5–3 m) long

DIET Grass, leaves, and shrubs

HABITAT Deserts

DISTRIBUTION Eastern Asia

Greater mouse deer
Tragulus napu

The greater mouse deer is tiny, with short, pencil-thin legs. When alarmed, it stamps one or both hind feet on the ground, to which other individuals may respond by stamping back.

SIZE 12–14 in (30–35 cm) long

DIET Leaves, flowers, and other vegetation

HABITAT Tropical forests

DISTRIBUTION Southeast Asia

White patch on chin and throat

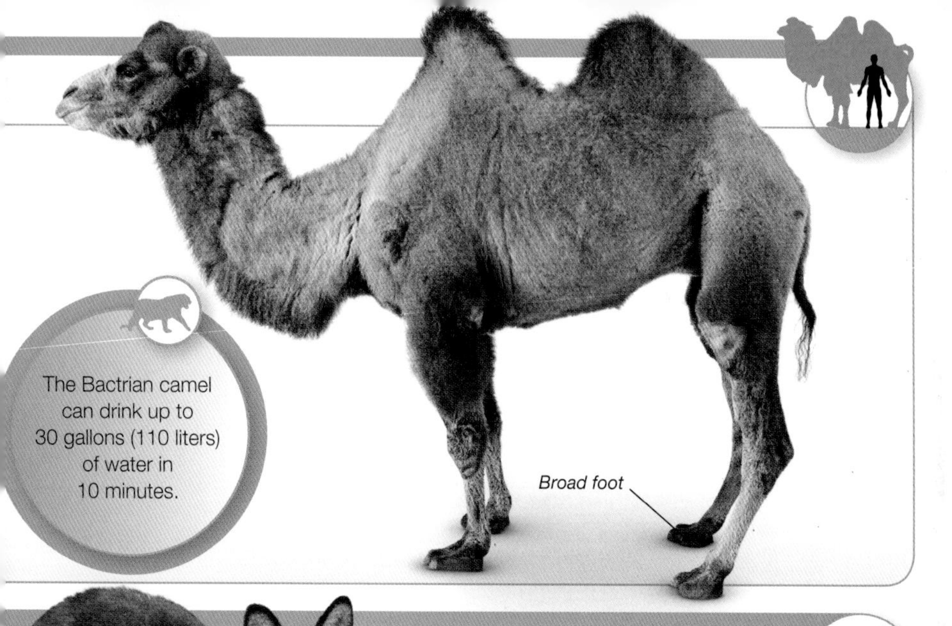

Alpine musk deer

Moschus chrysogaster

ENDANGERED

Although they resemble deer, like the mouse deer, musk deer lack antlers and are not true deer. Males have a scent gland, called the musk pod, near the rump. The scent (musk) made by the gland helps them to attract mates. Humans hunt this animal and use its scent to make perfumes, soaps, and medicines.

SIZE 27½–39 in (70–100 cm) long

DIET Grass, shrubs, leaves, and shoots

HABITAT Forests and mountains

DISTRIBUTION Southern Asia

Giraffe
Giraffa camelopardalis

The long neck of the giraffe makes it the tallest mammal on land. It helps the giraffe to feed on treetop leaves that cannot be reached by any other hoofed mammal. Male giraffes also use their necks to fight one another.

Neck can grow up to 6½ ft (2 m) in length

SIZE 12½–15½ ft (3.8–4.7 m) long

DIET Mainly acacia leaves and wild apricot

HABITAT Dry savanna and open woodlands

DISTRIBUTION Sub-Saharan Africa

Giraffes go into a deep sleep for only 20 minutes at a time.

Caribou
Rangifer tarandus

Also known as reindeer, this Arctic species forms huge herds of up to half a million animals in the spring. In April they migrate northward to spend the summer in the Arctic tundra. In the winter, the herds form smaller groups and move southward to warmer areas.

Okapi
Okapia johnstoni

This close relative of the giraffe has a tongue that is 14 in (35 cm) long—useful for curling around leaves and drawing them into its mouth to eat, and for licking and cleaning its eyes.

SIZE 6½–7 ft (2–2.2 m) long

DIET Leaves and shoots

HABITAT Rain forests

DISTRIBUTION Central Africa

SIZE 4–7 ft (1.2–2.2 m) long

DIET Grass, sedges, herbs, moss, and lichens

HABITAT Polar regions, mountains, and temperate forests

DISTRIBUTION North America, Europe, and Asia

Moose

Alces alces

The large antlers of the male moose take about 3–4 months to grow to their full size. Like all deer, its antlers fall off at the end of the breeding season and are replaced by new ones the next season.

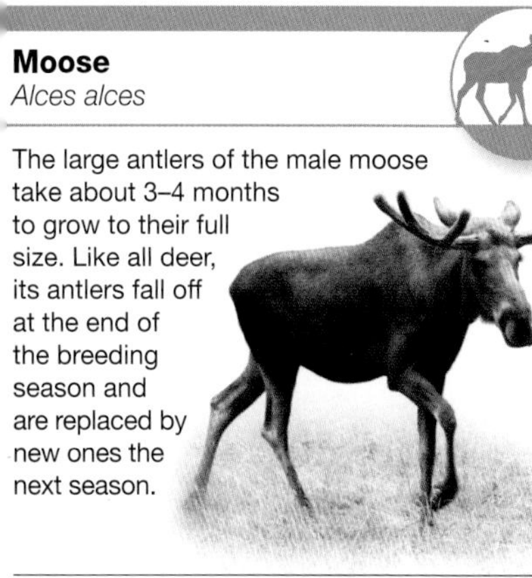

SIZE 8¼–11½ ft (2.5–3.5 m) long

DIET Shoots, stems, and roots of plants

HABITAT Forests, woodlands, and wetlands

DISTRIBUTION North America, Europe, and Asia

Pronghorn

Antilocapra americana

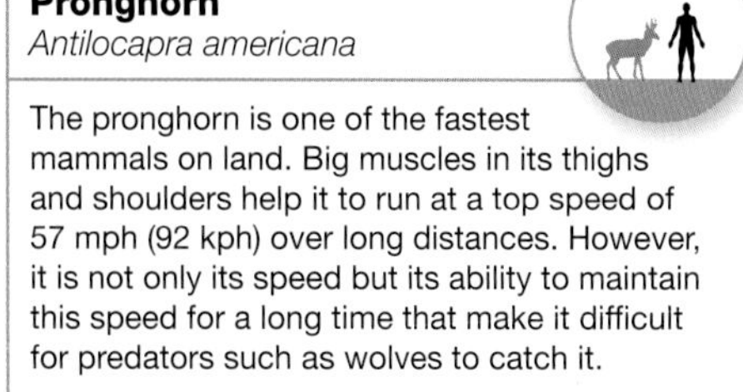

The pronghorn is one of the fastest mammals on land. Big muscles in its thighs and shoulders help it to run at a top speed of 57 mph (92 kph) over long distances. However, it is not only its speed but its ability to maintain this speed for a long time that make it difficult for predators such as wolves to catch it.

SIZE 3½–5 ft (1–1.5 m) long

DIET Grass, shrubs, and cactus

HABITAT Grasslands, deserts, and foothills

DISTRIBUTION Western and central North America

Asian water buffalo
Bubalus bubalis

ENDANGERED

This domestic animal is found in hot regions in Asia and spends the hottest part of the day resting in water or muddy pools. This helps it to keep cool and also get rid of flies and insects that live on its skin.

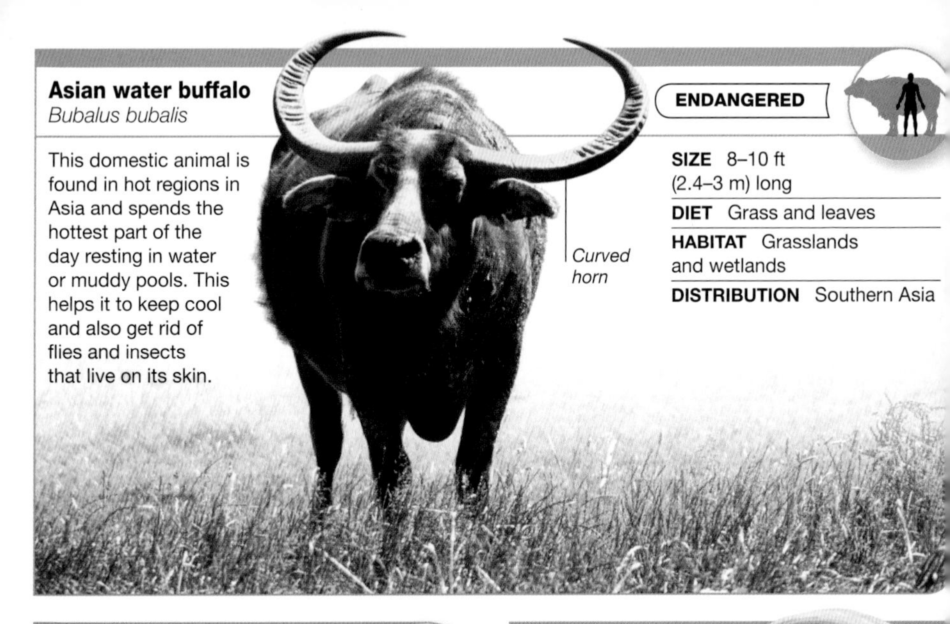

SIZE 8–10 ft (2.4–3 m) long

DIET Grass and leaves

HABITAT Grasslands and wetlands

DISTRIBUTION Southern Asia

Yak
Bos mutus

The yak has a two-layered hairy coat on its body. The outer layer is made up of long and waterproof hairs that help to keep the yak dry, while the undercoat is woolly and traps air to keep the yak warm.

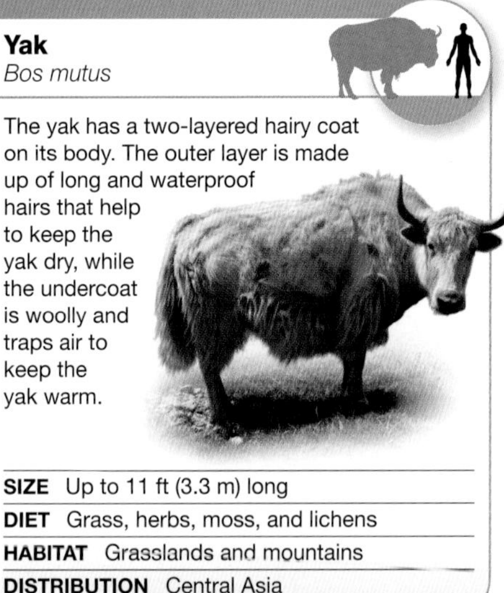

SIZE Up to 11 ft (3.3 m) long

DIET Grass, herbs, moss, and lichens

HABITAT Grasslands and mountains

DISTRIBUTION Central Asia

Domestic cow
Bos taurus

Cattle, or cows, were domesticated around 10,500 years ago and are an important part of livestock today. The Texas longhorn was once a popular breed of cattle in the US, but not many are seen today.

SIZE 4–5 ft (1.2–1.5 m) long

DIET Mainly grass

HABITAT Human settlements

DISTRIBUTION Worldwide except tropical forests and polar regions

American bison
Bison bison

Infant bison spend a lot of time play-fighting, which helps to hone the fighting skills of the males and improve their strength. As the males mature, they leave the herd and form separate groups, returning to fight rival males in the breeding season. Males are highly aggressive and fight by ramming heads.

SIZE 7–11½ ft (2.1–3.5 m) long

DIET Grass, sedges, and plants

HABITAT Mountains, forests, and grasslands

DISTRIBUTION North America

Common waterbuck
Kobus ellipsiprymnus

This antelope's skin gives off an oily musklike scent. Although this scent helps the animal to locate other waterbucks, it also makes it easy for predators to find this antelope.

SIZE 4¼–8 ft (1.3–2.4 m) long

DIET Grass and leaves

HABITAT Savanna and woodlands

DISTRIBUTION East Africa

White markings on rump

Sable antelope
Hippotragus niger

Infant males have chestnut-colored fur on their body. As they grow older, the fur turns black. Females have chestnut to dark-brown fur all their lives.

SIZE 6¼–9 ft (1.9–2.7 m) long

DIET Grass and leaves

HABITAT Grasslands and savanna

DISTRIBUTION East to southeastern Africa

Blackbuck
Antilope cervicapra

Gemsbok

Oryx gazella

The gemsbok is found in some hot, dry parts of Africa. To avoid the daytime heat, this antelope grazes only at night or twilight. At noon groups of gemsboks huddle together in shaded areas.

SIZE 5¼–8 ft (1.6–2.4 m) long

DIET Grass, shrubs, and fruit

HABITAT Deserts, grasslands, and bushlands

DISTRIBUTION Southwestern Africa

A male blackbuck defends its territory aggressively against rivals. Fights are usually made up of short clashes between two rivals, and these clashes may go on for a number of days until one male gives way.

SIZE 4 ft (1.2 m) long

DIET Mainly grass

HABITAT Tropical forests and grasslands

DISTRIBUTION Southern Asia

Klipspringer

Oreotragus oreotragus

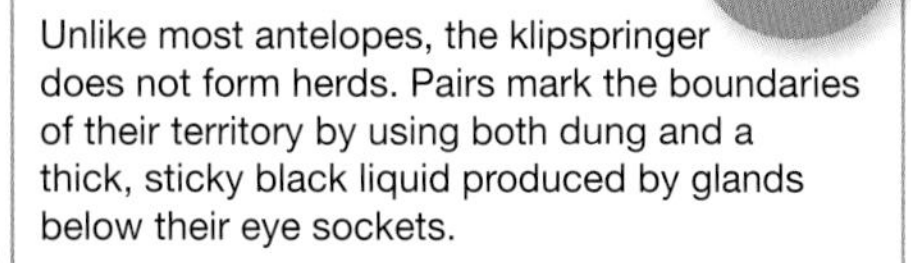

Unlike most antelopes, the klipspringer does not form herds. Pairs mark the boundaries of their territory by using both dung and a thick, sticky black liquid produced by glands below their eye sockets.

SIZE 2½–4 ft (0.8–1.2 m) long

DIET Mainly shrubs

HABITAT Mountains

DISTRIBUTION East, central, and southern Africa

Gland produces sticky liquid

Thomson's gazelle

Eudorcas thomsonii

When threatened, a Thomson's gazelle may escape by repeatedly jumping high into the air by arching its back and landing on all fours. These stiff-legged leaps, also known as "stotting," may startle and confuse the predator giving chase.

SIZE 3–4 ft (0.9–1.2 m) long

DIET Mainly grass

HABITAT Grasslands

DISTRIBUTION East Africa

Alpine ibex

Capra ibex

Herds of this mountain goat live in the European Alps. Male ibexes fight with rivals for the right to dominate a herd. During a fight, opponents rear up on their hind feet and lunge forward to clash horns with jarring force.

Thick, curved horn

SIZE 4–5½ ft (1.2–1.7 m) long

DIET Grass, buds, and shoots

HABITAT Open, rocky mountains

DISTRIBUTION The European Alps

Bighorn sheep
Ovis canadensis

A male's horns may weigh as much as the rest of its skeleton

The cloven hooves of the bighorn sheep have rough undersides. This allows the mammal to easily climb up rocky cliffs and hills, letting it escape from most predators that are unable to tackle such steep and slippery slopes.

SIZE 5–6 ft (1.5–1.8 m) long

DIET Mainly grass

HABITAT Mountains

DISTRIBUTION Southwestern Canada, western and central US, and northern Mexico

WILDEBEEST MIGRATION

Herds of wildebeest migrate across the Serengeti plains during the dry season in search of food and water. Along the way, they have to cross the wide Mara River. Nile crocodiles lie in wait in the Mara and ambush the wildebeest as they cross.

Each year, about 1.5 million wildebeest undertake a spectacular migration across Africa's Serengeti plains

Cetaceans

This extraordinary group of aquatic, air-breathing mammals includes about 85 species of whales, porpoises, and dolphins that form the order Cetacea. Their forelimbs are modified into flippers, helping them to steer as they swim.

FOCUS ON...
TYPES

Cetaceans can be classified in two groups based on the presence or absence of teeth.

▲ The baleen whales lack teeth and instead have plates of baleen hanging from their upper jaw. These plates are made of keratin and filter food, such as plankton, from the seawater.

▲ The toothed whales, such as this false killer whale, catch prey using their teeth.

Gray whale
Eschrichtius robustus

The gray whale is a baleen whale named after the gray patches on its skin. The head of a gray whale is covered in barnacles, and whale lice cling to its body wherever they can hold on. The whale lice feed on whale skin and damaged tissues, as well as scraps stuck to the whale's body.

SIZE 43–49 ft (13–15 m) long

DIET Invertebrates, such as worms, shrimp, and starfish

HABITAT Seas and oceans

DISTRIBUTION North Pacific

Bowhead whale

Balaena mysticetus

This baleen whale's bow-shaped head makes up about one-third of its total body weight. The whale uses its huge head to break through thick ice in the Arctic waters.

SIZE 46–59 ft (14–18 m) long

DIET Crustaceans and fish

HABITAT Seas, oceans, and polar regions

DISTRIBUTION Arctic and subarctic waters

Humpback whale

Megaptera novaeangliae

Humpback whales often hunt in groups. They surround a school of fish and one whale in the group blows a spiral of bubbles around the fish. Once enough fish are trapped in this "bubble net," the whales swallow them in large mouthfuls.

SIZE 43–46 ft (13–14 m) long

DIET Mainly krill and fish

HABITAT Coastal areas, seas, and oceans

DISTRIBUTION Worldwide except the Mediterranean Sea, Baltic Sea, Red Sea, and the Arabian Gulf

Blue whale

Balaenoptera musculus

ENDANGERED

The largest living animal on Earth, the blue whale has an equally massive appetite. It uses its baleen plates to filter-feed on more than 8,800 lb (4,000 kg) of food daily, but it doesn't eat at this rate throughout the year. It feeds only in the summer and can go without food during the winter.

SIZE 65½–98½ ft (20–30 m) long

DIET Mainly krill

HABITAT Seas and oceans

DISTRIBUTION Worldwide except the Mediterranean Sea, Baltic Sea, Red Sea, and the Arabian Gulf

Bottlenose dolphin

Tursiops truncatus

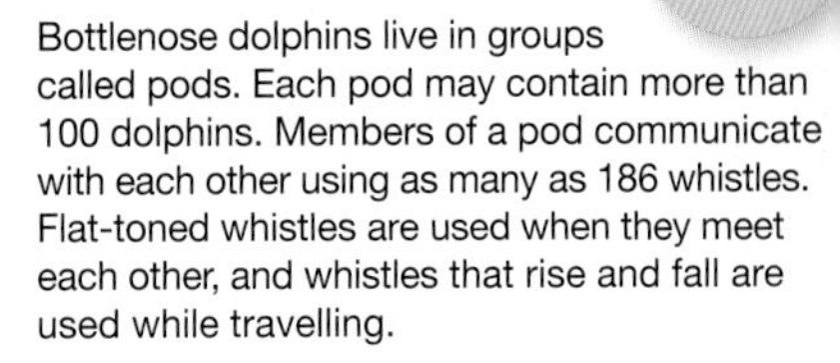

Bottlenose dolphins live in groups called pods. Each pod may contain more than 100 dolphins. Members of a pod communicate with each other using as many as 186 whistles. Flat-toned whistles are used when they meet each other, and whistles that rise and fall are used while travelling.

SIZE 6¼–13 ft (1.9–4 m) long

DIET Fish, mollusks, and crustaceans

HABITAT Coastal areas, seas, and oceans

DISTRIBUTION Worldwide except polar regions

Killer whale

Orcinus orca

Killer whales, or orcas, hunt together, killing prey in a number of ways. They may dislodge seals from floating ice by swimming together toward and under the ice to create large waves that tip the seals into the water. They may also take young seals from the shore.

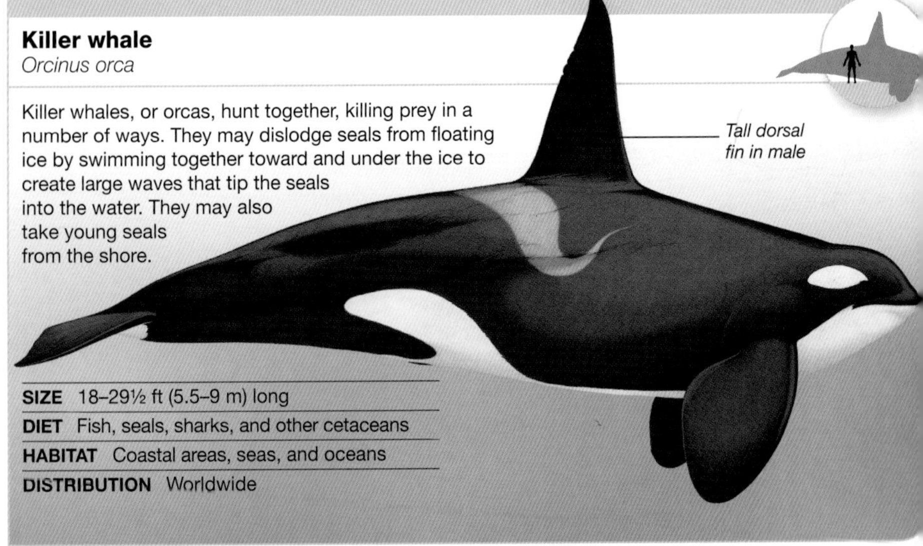

SIZE 18–29½ ft (5.5–9 m) long

DIET Fish, seals, sharks, and other cetaceans

HABITAT Coastal areas, seas, and oceans

DISTRIBUTION Worldwide

Cuvier's beaked whale

Ziphius cavirostris

Males of this species have a pair of small, cone-shaped teeth that protrude from the tip of their lower jaw. They use these teeth to bite and fight with each other for mates.

SIZE 23–24½ ft (7–7.5 m) long

DIET Mainly squid

HABITAT Seas and oceans

DISTRIBUTION Temperate and tropical waters worldwide

Cuvier's beaked whales can dive to depths of up to 6,200 ft (1,900 m).

Scars may be caused by parasites as well as in fights with rivals

Sperm whale

Physeter catodon

The sperm whale is the largest living toothed animal on Earth. Its lower jaw contains 20–26 conical teeth on each side. Each tooth is 8 in (20 cm) long—longer than the teeth of any other living predator.

SIZE 36–66 ft (11–20 m) long

DIET Mainly squid and octopuses

HABITAT Seas and oceans

DISTRIBUTION Deep waters worldwide except in Arctic waters

Head is one-third of total body size

Tail propels whale through the water

Amazon river dolphin

Inia geoffrensis

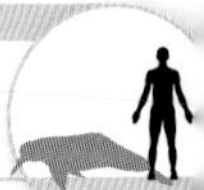

All dolphins are toothed. This species has poor eyesight and uses echolocation to locate prey and find its way in the muddy waters of its habitat. It emits high-pitched calls that travel through the water and bounce back from objects and animals in its path, creating a "picture" of its surroundings.

SIZE 6½–8½ ft (2–2.6 m) long

DIET Crabs, river turtles, fish, and shrimp

HABITAT Wetlands, rivers, and streams

DISTRIBUTION Amazon and Orinoco river basins in South America

Narwhal

Monodon monoceros

The male narwhal has one large tooth, or tusk, which can be as long as 10 ft (3 m). This toothed cetacean uses its tusk for display and to fight rival males during the mating season.

SIZE 13–14¾ ft (4–4.5 m) long

DIET Fish, mollusks, and crustaceans

HABITAT Coastal areas, seas, oceans, and polar regions

DISTRIBUTION Arctic Ocean

Harbor porpoise

Phocoena phocoena

True to its name, the harbor porpoise prefers shallow waters and is commonly seen in harbors and bays. Its numbers are falling because it often gets caught up in fishing nets in these areas. Water pollution also affects its population.

SIZE 4½–6½ ft (1.4–2 m) long

DIET Fish, squid, octopuses, and shellfish

HABITAT Coastal areas, seas, and oceans

DISTRIBUTION North Pacific, North Atlantic, and the Black Sea

Triangular, slightly sharklike dorsal fin

Common dolphins usually breathe no more than

3 times a minute

COMMON DOLPHINS

Common dolphins live in large groups called pods. Pod size may vary between several dozen to more than 1,000 members. These dolphins can often be seen jumping and splashing in water while making a variety of whistles and clicks.

Record breakers

FASTEST ON LAND

① A **cheetah** can run at a top speed of 71 mph (114 kph) to catch its prey.

② A **pronghorn** can sprint at 57 mph (92 kph) over long distances.

③ A **quarter horse** gallops at 50–55 mph (80–88 kph) and is the fastest breed of horse over short distances.

④ The slender legs of a **blue wildebeest** allow it to escape from predators at speeds of about 50 mph (80 kph).

⑤ In spite of weighing about 500 lb (226 kg), a **lion** can close in on its prey at speeds of up to 50 mph (80 kph).

HEAVIEST ON LAND

① A male **African savanna elephant** is the heaviest mammal on land and can weigh up to 13,000 lb (6,000 kg).

② A male **Asiatic elephant** weighs up to 12,000 lb (5,400 kg).

③ A **hippopotamus** weighs 7,000 lb (3,200 kg). Its skin alone weighs about half a ton.

④ The **African forest elephant** is the lightest species of elephant and weighs about 5,500 lb (2,500 kg).

⑤ A male **white rhinoceros** weighs 5,000 lb (2,300 kg).

FASTEST IN WATER

★ The **Commerson's dolphin** is the fastest aquatic mammal and can swim at a speed of 35 mph (56 kph).

★ A **Dall's porpoise** can surge through the water at a speed of 34 mph (55 kph).

★ The **blue whale** can move at a speed of 31 mph (50 kph) over short distances.

HEAVIEST IN WATER

★ The **blue whale** is the largest mammal on Earth and weighs up to 330,000 lb (150,000 kg).

★ A **bowhead whale** can weigh up to 177,000 lb (80,000 kg).

★ A **humpback whale** weighs up to 170,000 lb (77,000 kg).

LONGEST

Longest migration
\ gray whale migrates over '0,000–13,000 miles (16,000–?1,000 km) every year—this is he longest known migration among mammals.

In 1970, an album containing the songs of the humpback whale became a top-selling record in Europe and the US.

Longest song
Male humpback whales sing the ongest songs in the animal kingdom. Each of their songs lasts for about half an hour and may attract females, warn off rival males, or help to detect other whales.

Longest tongue
\ tube-lipped nectar bat has the longest ongue among mammals, relative to its body size. The bat is about 2 in (5 cm) long and its ongue measures 3 in (8.6 cm) in length.

♦ **Longest life span**
Some scientists think that bowhead whales have the longest mammal life span. They can live for more than 200 years.

♦ **Longest gestation**
An elephant carries its baby in its womb for a period of 22 months.

♦ **Longest hibernation**
An Alpine marmot hibernates for about nine months of the year and stays active for only three months.

♦ **Longest childhood**
Young orangutans spend close to 15 years of their life with their mothers, learning how to survive in the rain forest.

OTHER MAMMAL RECORDS

- The three-toed sloth is the **slowest land mammal**, with a top speed of just).15 mph (0.24 kph).

- Kitti's hog-nosed bat is the **smallest mammal by body length**. It is 1–1¼ in 29–33 mm) long.

- The blue whale is the **loudest mammal**. ts call can be heard from as far as 500 miles 300 km) away.

- Humans live in the **largest social groups**. More than 288,850 people live per square mile in the city of Manila in the Philippines.

- The African elephant is the **strongest mammal** on land. It can carry the weight of more than 130 adult humans.

- Giraffes are the **tallest mammals** on land, and also the tallest animals in the world. They can grow to a height of 19 ft (6 m).

Amazing mammals

SUPER SENSES

★ The **Philippine tarsier's** eyes are as big as its brain. Its eyes have 300,000 night-vision receptors.

★ **Bottlenose dolphins** have a sharp sense of hearing and can hear high-pitched sounds with a frequency of up to 150,000 Hz. Humans can only hear sounds up to 20,000 Hz.

★ Like most wolves, the **gray wolf** has a keen sense of smell and more than 250 million smell receptors. A human only has about 5 million smell receptors in the nose.

A star-nosed mole takes an average of 0.23 seconds to identify, capture, and eat its prey.

★ **Humans** have 10,000 taste buds and can identify sweet, bitter, sour, salty, and savory flavors.

★ The **star-nosed mole's** nose has 25,000 touch receptors that help it to find prey.

OLDEST MAMMALS

• The tiny, shrewlike ***Morganucodon*** lived 210 million years ago and is one of the earliest mammals. Like its reptile ancestors, it had a double-jaw joint and laid eggs.

• ***Megazostrodon*** lived 190 million years ago and looked similar to *Morganucodon*. It probably burrowed and ran like modern rats and shrews. Its short cheek teeth had triangular points and may have been used for cutting up insects.

• The egg-laying ***Teinolophos*** lived 125 million years ago and is a prehistoric ancestor of modern monotremes.

• Chipmunk-sized ***Sinodelphys*** lived about 125 million years ago and is thought to be closely related to the first marsupials. It had similar wrists, ankles, and front teeth, but it is not clear whether it had a pouch.

• Rat-sized ***Eomaia*** lived about 125 million years ago and is related to the first placental mammals.

MAMMALS IN MYTHS

★ In ancient Egypt, a jackal-headed god called **Anubis** was the most important god associated with death. Priests conducted rituals for the dead while wearing a mask with the face of Anubis.

★ The elephant-headed god **Ganesha** is an important mythical figure in India. He is also called the "Remover of all Obstacles" and people often pray to him before starting a new task.

★ In European mythology, **Fenrir** is a gigantic and terrible monster in the form of a wolf. He was chained by the gods when they learnt that one day he would be responsible for the destruction of the world.

★ According to Greek mythology, the **Nemean Lion** was a huge and terrifying creature with the strength of 10 ordinary lions. Weapons could not wound it and its tough claws could slash through any armor.

MAMMALS IN SPACE

★ In 1948, a **rhesus macaque** named Albert became the first animal to be sent into space, on board a V2 rocket.

★ A **monkey** named Yorick and 11 **mice** made a missile flight to a height of 236,000 ft (71,930 m) from the Hollomon Air Force base in New Mexico in 1951.

★ In 1952, two **Philippine monkeys** and two **white mice** were launched into space on board a US Aerobee rocket.

★ A **domestic dog** named Laika became the first animal to orbit Earth on the Soviet *Sputnik 2* spacecraft in 1957.

MAMMALS IN MOVIES

★ The 1992 Hollywood comedy *Beethoven* featured a St Bernard, a popular breed of **domestic dog**.

★ In 1993, a **killer whale** was featured in *Free Willy*, a popular family movie.

★ An **orangutan** played the lead in the 1996 Hollywood comedy *Dunston Checks In*.

★ The 2003 drama *Hidalgo* was about an **American mustang** (wild horse) that won several long-distance endurance races.

Glossary

Adaptation A feature that helps an animal to survive in its environment.

Antler A branching bony growth on the head of deer.

Aquatic Describes animals that live in or near water.

Bacteria Simple, single-celled living things that are the most abundant organisms on Earth.

Baleen A brushlike fringe that hangs from the upper jaws of some whales. The baleen strains food from water.

Breeding Producing offspring.

Camouflage Colors or patterns on an animal's skin or fur that allow it to blend with its surroundings.

Canine teeth Sharp-pointed teeth used for piercing and gripping prey.

Carcass The dead body of an animal.

Carnivore A mammal belonging to the order Carnivora, such as dogs. It is also used to describe any animal that eats mainly meat.

Carrion The remains of dead animals.

Cell One of the tiny units from which all living things are made.

Classification A method of identifying and grouping living things.

Cloaca An opening at the rear of egg-laying mammals. It is used for laying eggs and getting rid of waste.

Clotting A process that makes blood turn solid, sealing an open wound.

Colony A group of animals belonging to one species that live together.

Coniferous Cone-bearing plants, such as fir and pine trees. Most are evergreen and have simple leaves.

Crustacean A type of mainly aquatic invertebrate with two pairs of antennae.

Digestion A process that breaks down food into tiny particles that the body can absorb and use.

Domesticated An animal that has been tamed and lives fully or partly under human control.

Echolocation One way in which dolphins and bats find their way and locate food. It involves emitting sound signals and then listening for the echoes that bounce back.

Endangered Describes a species that is in danger of becoming extinct.

Evolution The mechanism by which life-forms change over many generations, becoming better suited to their environment. It often takes place over millions of years.

Extinct A species of plant or animal, such as the thylacine, that has died out.

Family A level in classification that is part of an order and contains closely related genera (singular, **genus**).

Flipper A paddlelike forelimb found in aquatic mammals, such as whales.

Forage To search for food.

Forelimbs The front legs of an animal.

Genus A group of species that share a unique feature or features.

Gestation The period of pregnancy between mating and birth, during which placental and pouched mammals develop inside the mother's womb.

Gland An organ that produces specific substances—such as scents—that have a particular purpose.

Grazer A herbivore that feeds on grass.

Herbivore An animal that grazes or browses on plants.

Hibernation The ability of some animals to lower their heart rate and body temperature and become inactive during colder months when food is in short supply.

Hind limbs The back legs of an animal.

Hoof The horny covering at the tip of an ungulate's foot.

Horn An unbranched, pointed, bony growth on the head of some hoofed animals that is covered with keratin.

Incisor teeth Teeth at the front of the mouth, usually used for biting and gnawing.

nsect An invertebrate vith three pairs of legs, sually two pairs of wings, nd a body divided into hree parts.

nvertebrate An animal vithout a backbone.

Ceratin The substance hat forms hair and the uter covering of hooves, laws, and most horns.

Crill A crustacean that orms the main food ource of baleen whales.

.arva An immature, ften wormlike, form that atches from the eggs f many insects and ther invertebrates.

.itter A group of young hat are all born to a emale mammal at one time.

Mammary glands Glands on the body of emale mammals that roduce milk for suckling he young.

Marine Related to the sea. Marine animals live n or around the sea.

Migration A journey made by an animal, often due to seasonal changes, in search of food, water, or good breeding conditions.

Molar teeth Teeth that can be flattened, ridged, or have sharp cutting edges, and are usually used for chewing.

Mollusk A soft-bodied invertebrate, such as a snail, which is usually protected by a hard shell.

Nectar A sugary liquid produced by flowers.

Nocturnal Animals that rest during the day and are active at night.

Offspring The young of an animal.

Omnivore An animal that feeds on a variety of food, including both plants and animals.

Order A group of closely related families.

Organ A body part, such as the heart, that performs a specific function in an organism.

Parasite An animal that lives on or inside the body of another species, known as the host. It feeds either on the host animal or on food the host has swallowed. It may weaken the host, and can kill it.

Placenta A temporary organ that develops inside the womb of many female mammals. It allows the exchange of nutrients and waste between the mother and developing young.

Predator An animal that hunts, kills, and eats other animals.

Prehensile Describes anything that is able to curl around objects and grip them.

Prey An animal that is hunted, killed, and eaten by a predator.

Reproduction A process through which a living thing produces young.

Roost The resting site of a flying animal.

Savanna A type of grassland found in hotter regions of the world, especially in Africa.

Scavenger An animal that feeds on dead remains and anything else it finds.

Scrubland A type of habitat dominated by shrubs and grass.

Sensory receptor Cells that help animals to see, smell, hear, taste, or touch.

Social Describes an animal that lives with others of its kind in a group.

Species A group of animals that can breed only with each other to produce fertile young.

Stalk To approach and track prey.

Suckle To feed on milk produced by glands in the mother's body.

Taiga Coniferous forests found in northern Eurasia.

Territory An area occupied by an animal or group of animals from which other members of the same species and gender may be excluded.

Tubers Short, fleshy underground stems or roots of some plants.

Tundra Barren, treeless region bordering Earth's polar regions and near the tops of mountains.

Tusk A type of tooth that sticks out of a mammal's mouth when the mouth is closed.

Ultrasound Sounds that are too high-pitched for human ears to detect.

Ungulate A hoofed mammal, such as a zebra (an odd-toed ungulate) or a pig (an even-toed ungulate).

Urinary system A body system that removes liquid waste from the body.

Vertebrate An animal with a backbone.

Wetland An area of land that remains flooded for most of the year.

Index

A

BC

DEF

GH

IJKL

MNO

PQRS

TUVWYZ

Acknowledgments

Dorling Kindersley would like to thank: Monica Byles for proofreading; Helen Peters for indexing; Saloni Talwar for editorial assistance; and Dhirendra Singh and Pankaj Bhatia for design assistance.

The publishers would also like to thank the following for their kind permission to reproduce their photographs:

(Key: a-above; b-below/bottom; c-center; f-far; l-left; r-right; t-top)

2–3 Corbis: Cyril Ruoso / JH Editorial / Minden Pictures. **4–5 Corbis:** Theo Allofs (b). **5 Fotolia:** s1000rr (cra). **8 Getty Images:** Manoj Shah / The Image Bank. **9 Corbis:** Image Source (bl). **FLPA:** Winfried Wisniewski (b). **10 Corbis:** Mitsuaki Iwago / Minden Pictures. **11 Corbis:** Michele Burgess (b). **Dreamstime.com:** Ben Mcleish (tr). **12 Dorling Kindersley:** Thomas Marent (clb). **13 Corbis:** Theo Allofs (crb). **Dreamstime.com:** Luna Vandoorne Vallejo (cra); Vladimir Melnik (tl); Pascalou95 (clb). **16 Dreamstime.com:** Nico Smit (bl). **17 Corbis:** Jo Prichard / epa (t). **Dreamstime.com:** Monika Habicher (bc); Jean-edouard Rozey (bl). **18–19 Corbis:** Katherine Feng / Minden Pictures. **20 Getty Images:** Andrew Watson / AWL Images. **21 Corbis:** David Watts / Visuals Unlimited (bc). **22–23 Corbis:** David Watts / Visuals Unlimited. **22 Corbis:** D. Parer & E. Parer-Cook / Auscape / Minden Pictures (br). **23 Alamy Images:** Dave Watts (br). **Corbis:** Martin Harvey (tc); David Watts / Visuals Unlimited (c). **25 Photoshot:** Bruce Beehler (tr). **26 Corbis:** Tobias Titz / fstop. **27 Ian Montgomery / Birdway.com.au** (bc). **28 Getty Images:** Carol Farneti Foster / Oxford Scientific (clb). **29 Corbis:** D. Parer & E. Parer-Cook / Auscape / Minden Pictures (tc, tr). **30 Corbis:** Pete Oxford / Minden Pictures (b). **31 Corbis:** SA Team / Foto Natura / Minden Pictures (br). **Getty Images:** Stephen J Krasemann / All Canada Photos (tr). **naturepl.com:** Luiz Claudio Marigo (bl). **32 Dreamstime.com:** Tamara Bauer (br). **32–33 Corbis:** Cyril Ruoso / JH Editorial / Minden Pictures (tc). **33 Dreamstime.com:** Callan Chesser (bl). FLPA: Martin B Withers (tr). **34 Corbis:** Mike Gillam / Auscape / Minden Pictures (bl); Martin Harvey (br). **35 Corbis:** Steve Kaufman (b). Photoshot: Daniel Heuclin (cl); A.N.T. Photo Library (cr). **36 Corbis:** Jean-Paul Ferrero / Auscape / Minden Pictures (tl). **37 Corbis:** Pete Oxford / Minden Pictures (tl). **Getty Images:** Visuals Unlimited, Inc. / Dave Watts (br). **38 Corbis:** Martin Harvey (br). **39 Corbis:** Gerry Ellis / Minden Pictures (br). **40–41 Corbis:** Shin Yoshino / Minden Pictures. **42 Getty Images. 43 Getty Images:** Juergen & Christine Sohns / Picture Press (bc). **45 Dreamstime.com:** Bonita Cheshier (bc); Wouter Tolenaars (tr). **46 Corbis:** HO / Reuters (b). **47 Corbis:** Pete Oxford / Minden Pictures (t). **Getty Images:** Tim Jackson / Oxford Scientific (b). **49 Getty Images:** Juergen Ritterbach / Photodisc (br). **50 Dorling Kindersley:** David Peart (l). **51 Corbis:** Luciano Candisani / Minden Pictures (b); Chris Newbert / Minden Pictures (t). **53 Alamy Images:** imagebroker (br). **54–55 Corbis:** Martin Harvey. **56–57 Corbis:** Kevin Schafer (t). **58 Corbis:** Kevin Schafer (bc). **58–59 Fotolia:** Eric Isselée (b). **59 Corbis:** Gerry Ellis / Minden Pictures (r). **60 Corbis:** Christian Helweg / National Geographic Society (br). **Dreamstime.com:** Gatito33 (bl). **61 Corbis:** Steven Kazlowski / Science Faction (br). **Dreamstime.com:** Martha Marks (bl). **63 Corbis:** Joe McDonald (t). **64 Getty Images:** Michael & Patricia Fogden / Minden Pictures (bl). **68–69 Alamy Images:** David Chapman. **70 FLPA:** Frans Lanting (cr). **71 Photoshot:** Nick Garbutt (tr); Daniel Heuclin (bl). **72 Dreamstime.com:** Lin Joe Yin (bl). **73 Corbis:** Thomas Marent / Minden Pictures (tl). **74–75 Dorling Kindersley:** Jerry Young (b). **75 Corbis:** Thomas Marent / Visuals Unlimited (br). **Dreamstime.com:** Lukas Blazek (tr). **77 Dreamstime.com:** Michael Lynch (br). **78 Corbis:** Eric and David Hosking (tr). **Dorling Kindersley:** Jamie Marshall (tl). **82–83 Corbis:** Kazuo Honzawa / Sebun Photo / amanaimages. **85 Corbis:** Stephen Dalton / Minden Pictures (br); Jean-Paul Ferrero / Auscape / Minden Pictures (bc). **86 Corbis:** Chase Swift (bc); Hugo Willocx / Foto Natura / Minden Pictures (br). **88–89 FLPA:** Christian Ziegler / Minden Pictures. **90 Dreamstime.com:** Mille19 (br). **Photoshot:** Photo Researchers (bl). **91 Dreamstime.com:** Martinsevcik (tl). **FLPA:** Frans Lanting (cra). **Getty Images:** Nigel Dennis / Gallo Images (b). **92 Dreamstime.com:** Dmitry Zhukov (tr). FLPA: Gregory Guida (b). **93 Corbis:** Ken Catania / Visuals Unlimited (clb). **Photoshot:** Daniel Heuclin (bl). **100–101 Corbis:** Alaska Stock. **102 Corbis:** Konrad Wothe / Minden Pictures (bl). **103 Corbis:** Tim Davis. **106 Dreamstime.com:** Moose Henderson (tc). **106–107 Dreamstime.com:** Jeanninebryan (b). **108–109 Corbis:** Ocean (b). **Dreamstime.com:** Nico Smit (t). **110 Getty Images**: Purestock (br). **112 Dreamstime.com:** Toneimage (b). **113 Corbis:** Tom Brakefield. **116–117 Corbis:** Daniel J. Cox. **118 Corbis:** Clem Haagner; Gallo Images (tl). **119 Dreamstime.com:** Nico Smit (b). **120 Dreamstime.com:** Lukas Blazek (br). **121 Dreamstime.com:** Vladimir Blinov (tr). **126 Photoshot:** Daniel Heuclin (br). **127 fotoLibra:** Jonathan Mitchell / Lightroom Photos (bl). **128 Dreamstime.com:** Vasiliy Vishnevskiy (l). **128–129 Dreamstime.com:** Sdbower (t). **129 Dreamstime.com:** Julie Lubick (r). **130 Dreamstime.com:** Jakub Cejpek (bl). **131 Getty Images:** Fotosearch (b). **133 Dreamstime.com:** Jean-marc Strydom (br). **135 Dreamstime.com:** Twildlife. **136–137 Dreamstime.com:** Roman Murushkin. **138 Dreamstime.com:** Verdelho (tl). **142 Corbis:** Kevin Schafer / Minden Pictures. **144–145 Corbis:** Robert Harding Specialist Stock.

For further information see: www.dkimages.com